Be Still

Be Still

Simple Keys
to Living a
Spiritual Life
in a
Material World

by

Jim Fox

Published by
The Centre of the Labyrinth

First published and distributed in the United Kingdom by:

The Centre of the Labyrinth

The Centre, 1 Pell Street, Swansea, SA1 3ES

Tel.: (44) 1792 477123

www.thecentre-swansea.co.uk

A catalogue record for this book is available from the British Library

ISBN 978-0-9573855-0-4

This book is dedicated with gratitude
to the memory of
Violet & Trevor Reeves

Contents

1. The Beginning
2. A Parable
3. Today Is The Day
4. Connecting With The Energy
5. Who Am I? Who Should I Be?
6. Tree Meditation
7. A Positive Charge
8. Living In Abundance
9. The Law of Attraction
10. Why Meditate?
11. Oneness
12. Responsibility
13. Worship
14. The Puzzle
15. Fly Like An Eagle
16. Faith
17. Clearing Space
18. Seize The Day
19. Pillow Talk
20. But I Don't Understand
21. Raindrop Meditation
22. Tune In
23. Muddy Waters and Sowing Seeds
24. Be Willing To Receive
25. A Time of Unlearning
26. Automatic Transmission
27. At The Third Stroke
28. Respect The Value
29. Laughing Matters
30. Spirituality or Religion
31. Rest In Peace
32. Death Is Not The End
33. And Finally

1
THE BEGINNING

This book came about when a number of paths in my life seemed to converge, making it something that had to happen rather than something that I just wanted to happen.

Writing is something I have done since childhood, from putting together a primary school magazine, writing songs, theatre reviews, a number of plays and a couple of musicals and, more recently, articles for Labyrinth Holistic Magazine. These articles, together with public speaking engagements on holistic and spiritual subjects, added fuel to the fire in my belly that was telling me that I had something to share, that I felt could be of benefit to those who were looking for answers to their questions and solutions to their dilemmas.

Looking at the world around me I was aware of the immense dissatisfaction and disillusionment there was, and still is, in our society. My belief is that the only way we can bring about peace, contentment, satisfaction and fulfilment in the world is to bring it about in our own personal world first. And this can only be achieved when we, as individuals, realise our connection with the source energy, whether we know that energy as god, goddess, the universe, spirit, divine source or by any other name.

Having tried to walk a variety of spiritual pathways in my life, and finding that most of them only served to take me around in circles, I no longer wear any badge or label which would identify me with any particular faith or religion. As you will discover through some of the following pages, I don't actually like the concept of religion and I feel that it often results in being a substitute for true spirituality. However, you will notice that I draw inspiration, and take pleasure in quoting, from what have become regarded as sacred texts and the written words of spiritual leaders of the past. Amongst other sources you will find that I have used words from the Bible, the Tao Te Ching, Buddhist and Pagan writings. This is not because I follow any of these paths, but because it is my belief that there is an element of wisdom and truth that underlies all of these writings but none of them are to be taken as the infallible and indisputable "*truth*".

I doubt very much that you will learn anything new from reading this book, what I have to say has been said by many people in many different ways. You may have forgotten that you know it, it may have been put on the back-burner some time ago and you forgot that it was still simmering away there, and by reading this you may be reminded of it, but I'm pretty sure that the chances are that this is all stuff you know already. My hope is that the words, stories and experiences in this book will help to stir up what is in that pot on the back-burner and that you can bring it to life and taste of it and enjoy the benefits of it.

If I can help just one person, through the following pages, to find their own inner peace and to make a connection with the divine energy that is within each one of us, then I will consider this work to have been worth it. It is my hope, as I write these words, that someone reading them will be stirred to delve deeper, to ask questions and to find answers within themselves and to discover the oneness of all creation and the source of creation.

Each chapter is purposely kept short so that the reader can spend time to digest it and meditate upon it before moving on to the next topic. I don't recommend that you try to read the whole thing in one go, rather, take one chapter at a time and allow it to sink in and become part of your consciousness. You may want to treat it as a daily meditation book, whatever feels the most comfortable to you, but don't rush it – the main message here, as you will soon discover, is to **Be Still** and allow any truths that you may find in these pages to take root, to grow and to bear fruit. Some ideas and messages you may find cropping up in more than one chapter – this is intentional as I feel that repetition can often help to ensure that we allow these things to take root. So, take your time, dip in when you feel like it and experience the changes.

2
A PARABLE

There was once a very rich business man whose son was about to celebrate his coming of age. The father told his son that he could have anything that he liked as a present to mark this special occasion. All he had to do was to name his preferred gift and the father would see to it that he got what he wanted. Coming from such a rich family, the son had never gone without and had always had everything that he could possibly want, the best clothes, the best gadgets, state-of-the-art computer systems – there was nothing that he had ever been denied. The son thought for a while and decided that he would really like to have his own private aeroplane.

True to his word, when the boy's birthday came around, the father took him to a nearby airfield with its own flying school and presented him with his brand new private aeroplane. Over the coming months the son was free to come down to the airfield and learn all about the mechanics of this wonderful machine and how to fly it. The boy bought all the books about flying and aeroplanes that he could get his hands on, he watched films about aviation and would spend time listening to the stories and experiences of all the skilled pilots down at the airfield.

After about 6 months, the father took it upon himself to visit the airfield to see how his son was getting on with his wonderful present. When he got to the hangar, he found the boy sitting by the plane reading his aviation magazines.

"How are you enjoying your present" inquired the father.

"Oh, it's fantastic", replied the son and he started telling his father all about the plane and its technical specifications and what it was capable of.

"That's great," said the father, *"why don't you show me what you can do with it?"*

The boy looked a little concerned and nervous, but made his way over to the plane and climbed up into the cockpit. He flicked all the right switches and the plane's single engine roared into life. The aeroplane taxied out of the hangar and onto the tarmac. The young pilot then headed towards the runway where he opened the throttle and started to speed down the straight track ahead of him. The speed of the plane picked up as it raced down the runway but, as he approached the end of the strip, the son applied the brakes and the machine started to slow. At the end of the runway he turned around and taxied back towards the hangar where his father waited with a look of confusion.

The son got out of the plane and walked towards his father, *"What do you think?"* he asked.

"I don't understand," the father said, *"you have this fantastic machine, you know how it works, you understand all the mechanics, you know everything that it is capable of, yet you are only using it to go up and down the runway. Why didn't you pull on the stick and take off? Why didn't you fly into the clouds instead of staying on the ground? What's the*

point of knowing all that you know if you aren't going to experience it for yourself?"

Hesitatingly the son replied, *"Maybe one day"*.

3
TODAY IS THE DAY

How often do we put off doing things in our life, for whatever reason? Sometimes it is fear, lack of confidence, lack of conviction, lack of trust. Sometimes it is just pure laziness or lethargy; sometimes we just can't be bothered, so we put it off until another day.

Just like the young man with his new aeroplane in chapter one, many of us know the mechanics, we've read all the manuals, we've watched the DVDs and listened to the CDs, we've subscribed to the magazines and attended the conferences. We've listened to the experiences of others and been excited and inspired by their stories and testimonies. We know how it works and we know the benefits and limitless potential of living a full, abundant life, of rising above the mundane and living in spirit. Yet we have still not taken hold of the joy stick, pulled back and allowed ourselves to soar into realms beyond the earthbound, material world that we feel safe in.

We say,

"one day I'll be able to put aside all the things that bind me, that hold me back, that limit me."

"one day soon, when I have more time."

"one day, when the kids have grown up"

"one day, when I don't have to worry about "

"one day, when the time is right for me"

Let me tell you now, that day never comes. Tomorrow never comes. There is only ever one time and that time is now. Today is the day. Don't put it off any longer, make your decision today to move into new and higher realms, to move from doubt to certainty, from fear to trust, from sickness to health, from want to abundance. As the ancient psalmist said:

*"**This** is the day that the lord has made; I will rejoice and be glad in it"*

I used to be one of the world's greatest procrastinators; I'd always think the sun would shine tomorrow so I could do whatever it was that needed doing, then. My motto used to be *"why do today what you can put off until tomorrow"*.

For 25 years I was a professional musician, travelling throughout the UK and Scandinavia playing my tunes and singing my songs. One night, or rather about 2 o'clock in the morning, after a particularly long run of gigs and feeling pretty exhausted, I was happily driving through the English countryside, heading towards home in Wales. It was quite a foggy night and there was no lighting along the road and no visible moon or stars to shed light onto what was a very dark rural road. I often listen to audio books on CD when I'm driving and I guess it was one of those times when the subconscious was doing the driving. You know what it is like when you have travelled from A to B but have no real recollection of the journey; it has all been done on auto-pilot. I was very rudely awakened from my hypnotic state and catapulted back into awareness by the sight of a rabbit darting out from the side of the road, straight into my path.

I had always said that if that sort of thing ever happens, the best and most sensible thing to do, for the safety of your self, passengers and other road users, is to keep driving in a straight line and not try to avoid the animal. Whether it was the sudden shock of being brought back into the present or not, I don't really know, but I ignored all my principles and swerved the car to try not to hit the poor little rabbit.

It had been raining, which had left the roads in a greasy condition and the weight of all my amplification equipment piled up in the back ensured that when I put the brakes on, the car skidded and the rear end spun around and pulled me off the road. As I left the carriageway and the vehicle started to roll over I remember thinking *"It really is like they say, everything is in slow-motion!"* I also remember thinking that this wasn't the way I had planned on dying and that I hadn't been able to say goodbye to Kiera, my partner.

The car rolled over a couple of times before finally come to a halt on its side in a very dark and damp field. I don't actually recall getting out of the car, but I must have crawled through the shattered windscreen and managed to make my way up the bank and onto the side of the road. I was able to get the attention of a passing motorist who very kindly stopped and called the police. When the police arrived on the scene they couldn't believe that I had managed to get out and walk away from the vehicle which was totally beyond repair.

That incident had a massive effect on my life and on my attitude towards life. For a moment, I had thought that there would be no tomorrow for me, I can't say that I had been frightened that I was going to die; I just seemed to accept that this was the end. Obviously it wasn't, and I'm here today to tell the tale, but it really did make me aware of the fact that we can't count on tomorrow coming. That I needed to do whatever I had to do "in the moment", because the moment is really the only time we have to do things.

Be Still, just take this moment to listen to your breathing, to be aware of your breathing. Be aware of your pulse, of your heartbeat. Be aware that you are alive, and that you are alive now. And be aware that now is the only time you have.

You can talk and dream about tomorrow as much as you like, but tomorrow will always be the next day, it will never be today. This is the day.

4

CONNECTING WITH THE ENERGY

I have stood in many places over the years where the natural energy has been so strong and obvious, that it has been impossible to ignore its existence. In stone circles such as Avebury in Wiltshire and Castlerigg in Cumbria, where the earth energy is so powerful; on top of Mount Teide in the Canary Islands with the power of the volcano, still smoking and spouting sulphur; on the icy high ground of Norway feeling the purity of the air all around; and at Grenen, the most northerly point of Denmark, and without a doubt the most powerful experience I have ever had of the power and energy of the natural elements, where the two bodies of water, the Skagerrak and Kattegak meet with a crash of waves coming from two different directions. To stand in that water with one foot in one sea and the other foot in the other sea is an experience that I have no words to describe to you. If you ever get the opportunity to experience it for yourself, don't pass it up.

As I write this, I am sitting outside a small tea-room in the English Lake District, an area of outstanding beauty which manages to encapsulate all four elements of the material world. The lakes – water, the rich green countryside – earth, the windy fells – air, and the remnants of a volcanic age which helped to shape the lakes into the wonderful place that it is – the element of fire. And to add to that is a wonderful awareness of magic, or spirituality which seems to rise from the very core of the place. A closer look at the history of the area will reveal a past that is rich in something far deeper than the material.

Throughout this book I repeatedly speak about *"Being Still"* and *"connecting"* with the source energy, or spirit. I also suggest that this energy is not something which is separate from us but is something that we are all part of and one with.

So then, what is this energy and how do we realise a connection with it?

First of all we need to accept and be aware of this energy. I'm sure that we have all walked into a room and sensed the atmosphere, or the energy, whether it was good or bad. Perhaps we have picked up "bad-vibes" from someone whom we have met or come into contact with. Very often when we enter a sacred space, be it a church, temple, stone circle or a room set aside for spiritual activity we will notice the difference as we become aware of the energy. Although there was an occasion recently when the energy I experienced in a church was far from peaceful. The church in question had been the centre a 17th Century witch hunt that led to the eventual execution of a number of innocent individuals and, even after so many years it felt very dark and oppressive inside this church. My wife described it as like having a heavy weight pressing down and a tightening around the chest making it difficult to breathe easily. The energy that had been left from the horror of the past was still very real and powerful.

Energy is all around us at all times, it is in us, it is part of us and we are part of it. Not only do we generate energy, but we are also part of the energy that has been pulsating throughout eternity and, as quantum physics tells us, we actually are eternal energy. That is our nature. This energy is the Chi of Tai Chi, the Qi of Qigong, the Ki of Reiki, the Spirit or Divine Force of many spiritual paths.

I want you try a couple of little experiments for yourself in order for you to experience something of this energy. Firstly, I want you to extend your arms in front of you about a shoulder-width apart with palms facing each other, then bring them together quickly and clap your hands. Now, repeat the action of extending your arms with palms facing, but this time I want you to be aware of the space between your hands and the energy held there. As you now move your hands together very, very slowly be aware of the strength of the energy between your hands. You will probably feel something of a resistance as your hands move closer together, something like the resistance when two magnets come together with the same poles facing each other.

You can move on to try some more experiments with a second person. Stand with your palms facing those of your partner, it doesn't matter whether you use one hand each or both hands at the same time. Be aware of, and feel the energy between the two of you. Once you are satisfied that you can feel each other's energy, stand with a distance of about 3 metres between you, now I want one of you to imagine that you are extending your field of energy as far as you can away from your physical body. When you feel that you are ready you can ask your partner to hold out their hand and slowly move towards you and then stop when they begin to feel that they have encountered your field of energy. This is something you can continue to do, noting all the time how much further you are able to extend your own energy field.

Now let's try and reverse that process.

Have you ever felt that sensation when you are sure someone is looking at you behind your back? You can't see them but you are aware of their eyes piercing into your skull? Here's another experiment you can try when you are sitting on a bus, a train, in the cinema or in a restaurant. Fix your gaze on the back of somebody's head, somebody sitting a few feet away in front of you, concentrate on sending your energy to reach them and see how long it is before they turn around because they have "felt" you looking at them.

We all have our own personal energy field, which is one of the reasons it can be uncomfortable when somebody "*invades*" that space, but, and here is the important thing, the experiments you have tried, or will try, show that we can extend or retract that energy as and when we desire.

I remember, many years ago, having a strange experience which at the time slightly freaked me out. A friend who had been studying Tai Chi asked me to relax while she stood behind me and placed her fingers on the back of my shoulder. It was the weirdest sensation as I felt her fingers actually pass through my skin and muscles and into my back as if she was performing an operation on me. I didn't see her do this as I had my back to her, but I did feel it, I really did feel it. Now, I think I'm right in assuming that it wasn't actually her hand that was passing through my skin and bone into my body but rather it was her "energy" that was penetrating my body mass.

I don't want to get deep into the realms of quantum physics here, but the scientific fact is that everything that exists is made of atoms, which in turn contain protons, neutrons and electrons, and it is the frequency at which these particles vibrate that makes things what they are, be it a table, a rock, a bone, skin or whatever material thing it appears as to us. In order for these particles to vibrate there is an enormous amount of space within each atom, in fact somewhere in the region of 98 – 99% of the atom is empty space. Everything, including us as human beings, is actually 98-99% empty space. Now I know there is a lot more to it than that, and this book is not the place to examine the subject in detail, but the above related experience is somewhat easier to understand, or believe, when we realise that we are basically empty space.

There are no barriers or limits to the energy that we all have and share, in much the same way that radio waves can pass through solid walls and still be received, so this life energy that we are part of is not restricted by any *"thing"*. Many holistic therapists and healers will use what they term *"distance healing"* which is quite simply an extending of energy, directing it to the person, wherever they might be, in order for them to receive the energetic boost that will aid their healing.

Taking this a step further, I would like to suggest that this energy does not belong to us as individuals and indeed does not actually emanate from us as individuals. It is my belief that all these separate energies are in fact one energy. Earth energy, water energy, fire energy, air energy, spirit energy, human energy, plant energy, any energy you care to name, are all one and the same energy.

Imagine, if you can, a group of people all standing in the middle of a stone circle. It is a stormy evening, the wind is blowing, the thunder is cracking and the lightning is flashing. Try to picture the energies shining out from each person, much like the old porridge adverts. Now visualise the energy of the stones and of the thunder and lightning and the rain, and you will see that it is impossible to distinguish one energy from another, as all those energies join and intermingle. You see, we talk about becoming one with nature, or one with a particular place or person, when in reality we are already one with everything and everyone. The separateness is just an illusion. And if we see this energy as being the life force, the source, the divine or even "god", we can also understand that we are one with this energy. The lie that we are separate from god and therefore need a saviour to reconcile us is just that – a lie. We are already one with god. We always have been and we always will be.

Just one more step and we can put a name to this energy. This energy doesn't take anything, it just gives. It gives life, it gives sustenance, it gives warmth, it gives a sense of belonging, it gives purpose, it gives peace, it gives and keeps giving but neither asks nor expects anything in return. It gives unconditionally. Its name? Love. And we, in our incarnation as human beings, are one with this energy, with love.

So when I ask you to **Be Still,** I am asking you to be aware of this oneness, to be aware of your connection to this energy, to be aware of this state of being "*in*" love. And as we become aware of this, our natural state, we allow ourselves to live in love and to flow with love. This is fulfilment. This is bliss. This is enlightenment.

5

WHO AM I?
WHO SHOULD I BE?

The human species is a strange one, not content to be what we are or to let others be what they are. We try to change ourselves and to change those around us.

I've always been something of a rebel, a non-conformist, some might say a free-spirit. Even as a child I had my own mind, which would often get me into trouble, I have to say. I knew what I wanted, I would eat the food I wanted to eat, wear the clothes I wanted to wear and do what I wanted to do – or at least, that was my intention. My parents and teachers, however, had other intentions. Right up until the age of 28, even though in my heart I would know what I wanted and what direction I should go in, I allowed my life to be governed by what others wanted for me.

My brother and I were totally different as children; he always had to work hard to achieve things at school. I remember that he would come home from school, have his tea, then go up to his room to do his homework, and usually that was the last we would see of him until supper. He worked hard, passed the 11plus, moved on to grammar school and got his qualifications. I, on the other hand, was totally different. I never had to work hard to get my grades, I never did any homework, in my early years at school I would usually finish in the top 3 in my class but I never understood why I had to study things that I had no interest in and which I knew I would never use in later life. Having a brother who worked and studied hard was a major problem too. I would often hear, *"Why can't you be more like Graham? Why don't you take school seriously? You'll end up sweeping the roads if you don't pass your exams, that's all you will be good for."* That was enough for me; my reaction was to take school even less seriously, do less work (if that was possible) and to have fun. I made sure that I didn't pass the 11 plus exam which would determine the type of high school that I would go on to and so went to the local Secondary Modern school with all my friends rather than to the Grammar School with all the swots and boring kids.

At the age of 15, when I had an idea of the subjects that would be of most use to me in later life I went on to Technical College and studied English and business studies – things that have been, and still are, a huge benefit to me in life. Graham went on to be very successful in his chosen field, but not without having to endure a great deal of stress along the way and so I can honestly say that I would not exchange my life for his in any way. What was right and good for him was not what was right and good for me.

I remember as well the *"summer of love"* in 1967, I was 14 and the whole hippy and flower power movement really resonated with me. Unfortunately I was just that little bit too young to be involved fully. Apart from that, my father would have blown a gasket if he knew what I was secretly doing. I would leave the house in the morning at weekends or in the evening with a bag containing all my "*hippy*" clothes, complete with round John Lennon style dark glasses, beads and a bell to hang around my neck. I would then find somewhere to change and be what I wanted to be for a few hours before having to change back into my conventional clothes without my father seeing me.

From a very early age, my biggest desire was to perform. I wanted to show off, to be in plays, to sing on the stage – I knew this was part of my destiny. At the age of 17 I sent away to various Drama Schools for information about enrolment only to have this totally dismissed by my parents. According to them this was not the sort of career that would bring security and stability for the future, the fact that it might bring satisfaction did not seem to matter to them and so I was not allowed to pursue this path. They wanted me to be what they wanted me to be, not what I wanted. And so, after a somewhat rebellious childhood, I started to conform.

A similar thing happened during my first marriage, I desperately wanted to be a singer and songwriter but I had a young family and so it was made very clear to me that such a life style would not bring stability and security. I had responsibilities and therefore had to put my own dreams and desires aside and be what other people wanted me to be. Years later, after some important changes to my life, I was able to become a relatively successful professional musician and I also got to work in the theatre, both as a performer and also as a writer and director, seeing a number of my own plays and musicals performed on the stage.

My family, my school teachers, even my spiritual leaders all tried to make my plans for me, believing that they knew what was best for me. As a result of listening to them I experienced much frustration and unhappiness over the years, until I allowed that rebellious, non-conformist child that still lived inside me to come to the surface again and live.

If you are reading this and you are a parent, teacher, pastor or have responsibility for others in any capacity, I would urge you to encourage them to find out what it is that they want for their lives rather than pushing them into a direction that you think is right for them. We all need to find our own dharma, or purpose in life and then to step out of the boundaries and plans that others have made for us and start living the life that is ours. When somebody tells you that you should be this or that, don't listen to them. When they tell you that you should go here or there or do this thing or the other thing, ignore them. The only person you have to be is yourself.

Now, before we start blaming everybody else for us missing the target, very often we are as much to blame ourselves. How often have we looked at those we admire or even idolise and said "I wish I could be like them"? The truth is you don't need to be like them, in fact you can never be like them. You are you. You are unique and special. You were meant to be you. You have your own dharma that only you can fulfil. Imagine the universe to be a jig-saw and there is a piece that needs to fit in at a certain position and you are that jig-saw piece. Nobody else can fit into that space and there is no other space that you can fit into. When you see somebody that is living a positive, spiritual life, a life of value and inspiration, don't look at them and say *"I want to be like you"*; when you see someone who appears to have all the things in their life that you would like, don't look at them and say *"I want my life to be like yours"*. The only person you need to be is you. The only life you need to live is your life.

A giraffe doesn't say *"I want to be a tiger"*. A bee doesn't look at a dog and say, *"I want to be like you"*. An oak tree doesn't say *"I wish I could be a daffodil"*. We are what we are and we are who we are. When we took on this incarnation it was because it was the right incarnation, the right life, the right existence.

Be Still, go deep into your heart and listen to who you really are, what you really want to be doing with your life and give yourself permission to be that person. Claim the freedom to be you. Think, as well, of anyone that you might be hindering from being who they really are. Set them free and allow them to fulfil their purpose, their dharma. You might be surprised to discover how liberating it is for yourself to allow another their liberty.

6

TREE MEDITATION

It is your dharma to be who you are and to live the life that you were meant to live, not anybody else's life, nor the life that anybody else wants you to live, but your life.

How do you find out what your own personal dharma or purpose is? The answer is to be found by acting upon two simple words, **Be Still**.

Note: With this meditation, and other meditations in this book, you might find it useful to speak it into a voice recorder, leaving plenty of appropriate pauses. Then play it back when you are ready to practice the meditation. This way, you are likely to get more out of the exercise than by just simply reading it.

Find a place where you won't be disturbed for a few minutes and stand with your legs about a shoulder's width apart, with your knees slightly bent so that there is some bounce in your body. You need to be comfortable and not rigid. Close your eyes and breathe slowly.

Begin by taking deep, slow breaths, relaxing all the time with each breath. Allow any tension to drain through your body and into the floor through your feet, all the time breathing slowly and evenly and deeply. As you breathe slowly, allow your body to relax, from your head right down to your feet, being aware of each muscle relaxing as you continue to breathe slowly. Once you feel calm and relaxed I want you to be aware of the floor beneath your feet and to imagine that you are a young tree, a sapling, just beginning its life. I want you to imagine that there are roots coming from the soles of your feet and reaching into the earth. As they reach down into the earth, they are searching out all the goodness in the soil, all the nutrients that help to bring growth and strength to the tree. Imagine those roots really spreading out into the earth below you, making a connection with the energy source. And as you stand there, imagine the gentle rain falling on you and around you, enriching the earth as you draw up the energy into your trunk and branches. Each time you breathe in, more energy enters into you and you start to become aware of the growing strength and energy flowing into your body, into your trunk. Imagine that energy, slowly travelling up into the trunk of the tree, and as it does, so you begin to feel the strength building up inside.

Then imagine the sun shining on you, bringing warmth to you as you grow. Be aware of that energy and that strength as you continue to grow, branches start to slowly grow, reaching to the sky, to the sun and you now start to feel energy entering into you from above as well as from below. And as the branches of the tree begin to grow and strengthen, direct your mind to the leaves beginning to appear on the branches. All the time staying aware of the energy flowing into you from below and from above, from the goodness of the earth and the warmth of the sun. You just have to stand there and receive that energy, and without trying or striving, your branches extend and the leaves continue to appear until you are a flourishing, leaf- covered tree. You don't have to think about making the leaves grow, they just grow, covering you with their greenness and soaking up the energy from the sun as your roots soak up the energy from the earth.

I want you to imagine as well that you can feel the elements around you as the weather continues to change. The rain falling onto you, the wind blowing against you. And as the wind gets stronger you allow yourself to sway and to bend with the wind. You don't try and resist it or fight it, you allow yourself to go with the strength of the wind, which in turn makes you stronger.

And as you stand there, just being a tree, the growth continues. Blossom starts to appear amongst the leaves, which in turn transforms into beautiful, nourishing fruit. Without striving or putting any effort into it, you are aware of the fruit growing on your branches. Fruit that will be shared and enjoyed by the animals and the humans who partake of it. Fruit that will not only give sustenance to those who eat it, but will also provide the seeds to produce more trees. Some of your fruit will simply fall to the ground, but even this fruit can transform. As the fruit lies on the earth, seemingly wasted, the seeds contained in it start to germinate and new life will emerge – new trees, new branches, new leaves and new fruit. Consider how you, as a tree, share your energy with the world, through the abundance of your fruit.

As a tree, you continue to grow taller and stronger, you continue to produce leaves and fruit and all you have to do is be the tree. You don't have to work at being a tree, you don't have to strive to grow leaves, you don't have to force the fruit to appear, you just "be" the tree and all these things happen. It is the nature of the tree, the dharma of the tree.

Now, just before you come back, I want you to consider how easy this has all been, from the sending down of the roots through to the growing of the stem and the trunk, the branches reaching out to the sun, the leaves and blossom appearing, the fruit growing, maturing and ripening, and the new life emerging. As a tree, you have not had to force anything, you have not had to strain, you have not had to worry or strive to produce this growth and this abundance of leaves and fruit. You have not had to concern yourself about the other trees, or whether there will be other trees after you as your fruit and seeds will take care of that. All you have had to do is to be a tree.

Now it is time to come back to your human state, but bring with you all that you have learnt and experienced as a tree, and know that in order to fulfil your purpose, your dharma, all you have to do is to be. You don't need to stress, you don't need to strive, you don't need to concern yourself about anything, you just need to be.

Be still. Be a tree.

7

A POSITIVE CHARGE

I had wonderful parents, and although they were never particularly wealthy, we never went without in any way. Both my father and my mother worked hard to be able to provide us with good food, good clothes, a nice home and at least one holiday a year. I was the baby of the family and shared my childhood with my brother. Mum and Dad's first child, Glenys, sadly only lived for 12 months and, although I never knew her she was still very much a part of our family. Whether it was because they had lost a baby at such an early age or not, I don't really know, but I remember my mother as being particularly protective when I was a small child. One area where she was perhaps a little over-protective was that I was never allowed to climb anything, whether it was a tree or a climbing frame or any other structure that would tempt me from the safety of having my feet on the ground. I can still hear her words if I was to attempt climbing anything, "*If you climb up there, you are going to fall*". It wasn't even just a possibility, it was definite. There was no "*you **might** fall*", there was no doubt about it, I was going to fall.

Guess what, all these years later I still have a fear of heights, the belief that I am going to fall makes me physically feel ill. I can't climb a ladder, even a step ladder makes me feel dizzy, in fact, I don't even like standing on a chair to change a light-bulb. I allowed those negative words to take root in me and as a result I have missed out on so many wonders. Never being able to stand on the edge of a cliff and appreciate what that must feel like, never being able to experience the sensations of floating in a hot air balloon or gliding to earth under the canopy of a parachute.

When I was 11 years old, I was being taught in school science lessons the different theories about the creation of the universe. I remember one particular lesson where we discussed the theory that the existence of the earth was due to a massive solar explosion. In those days our religious education lessons were based solely on the bible, we didn't learn about other religions, everything was taught from a Christian angle. Once, in a lesson about Genesis and creation I suggested to the teacher that, if what we were learning in the science class had any basis, maybe we should be worshipping the sun as that was our source. I was reprimanded for being disruptive and was told that *"with an attitude like that you will probably commit suicide by the time you are 21"*, presumably because if I didn't share his belief I would have nothing to live for. What an awful thing to say to anyone, let alone an impressionable 11 year old. Those words haunted me for a long time and I can tell you that I felt a great sense of relief when I finally reached the age of 22.

A number of years later, at a psychic and mystic fayre, I was informed by a palmist that the lines on my hands showed that I would never be wealthy and would always have money problems, and I believed her. For a long time I lived my life with those words firmly rooted in by beliefs. I never expected to have any money, so I didn't have any. I expected to be constantly struggling with finances and that's what happened, using credit cards and loans and allowing the debt to increase to such an extent, that all I ever seemed to be doing was paying off the interest and never getting to reduce the overall balance of my debts.

Let me be clear here, I'm not blaming anyone else, not my parents nor my teachers nor the palmist, the fact is that I allowed myself to be influenced by these negative comments. I allowed them to take root and grow. It was my responsibility and I let myself be affected.

Just think of all the negative things that have been said to you since childhood, or the things that you have said to your own children, your partner, your friends.

"You'll never amount to anything"

"Don't even bother trying out for the school choir with a voice like yours; you just don't have a voice"

"Don't pick him for the team, he's useless"

"Don't bother, you won't understand, it's too deep/complicated/intellectual for you".

"Don't go near the water, you'll drown"

"Children should be seen and not heard"

The two important lessons here are, firstly, that we don't allow ourselves to be touched by the negative things people say to us. Very often they don't have any malicious intent in what they say, believing that they are saying things for our own good and our protection. There are occasions of course when things are said with an intention to hurt, but whatever the reason behind the words it is our responsibility to use discernment and only allow the positive into our lives and consciousness. If someone tells you that you are not good enough – determine to prove them wrong. When you are told that you can't sing, take time to learn how to use your voice. As a musician, it is my belief that everyone has a voice which they can use to express themselves through song. Even people like Bob Dylan or Tom Waits do not have what would be described as a conventional singing voice, if they were to apply for the X-factor TV show they wouldn't get past the audition stage, yet what they have is their own unique voice which is able to convey the spirit and meaning of their words through song, in a way that nobody else can.

Many people who were written off at school for not having academic qualities and being unable to pass exams, have gone on to be leading business people and entrepreneurs making an incredible success of their lives. I really believe that too much emphasis and pressure is put on young people today to pass exams and gain qualifications. Life is not a competition, we are not meant to be striving to prove that we are better than someone else all the time. By putting 7 year-olds through the pressure and stress of an exam, and making those who may not do so well in that exam feel inferior to those who find the whole exam situation a breeze, can have a lasting negative effect on those children. The ones who do well are always under pressure to keep up that standard, and the ones who do not do so well are always under pressure to move up the table and beat others, in order to get a higher position.

I know that there are those who would argue that such competition is good practise for coping with the "*real*" world and that children should learn to be able to cope with failure or "*coming second*", but the so-called *"real"* world doesn't have to be like that. If we could teach our children from an early age that life doesn't need to be competitive, that the important thing is that we live our lives in the way that is right for us, without trampling over others to reach our goals. By being mindful of everybody's equally important individual role and place in the greater picture, we might be on our way to producing a better, more caring, supportive and understanding society. In the words of Grantland Rice, the early 20th Century sportswriter, *"For when the great scorer comes to write against your name, He marks not that you won or lost but how you played the game."*

Secondly, and just as important, we need to be mindful of the things that we say to others. Our words can either build up and edify a person or they can deflate and even destroy. What we say in just a few seconds can have a lifetime effect on the hearer. The old saying, *"sticks and stones may break my bones, but words can never hurt me"*, is simply not true. A life can be ruined by the words that someone says.

If you have children of your own, or if you have close contact with children, either in a professional or a family setting, don't ever put those children down. Don't tell them that they are not as good as someone else, or even that they are better than someone else, just praise and encourage them for being who and what they are. Allow them to be themselves, not what you want them to be. Allow them to excel and grow in what they are naturally good at, rather than pushing them in areas where they are not comfortable or have no interest. Don't ever tell them that they are no good or that they are failures.

With those you work with or come into contact with on a daily basis, look for things that you can comment on which will make them feel good and appreciated. Find things to compliment, things to praise. Make it your mission to say only words that encourage and build up, to communicate positivity at every opportunity. If you don't have something positive to say, say nothing.

Be Still. Look within and root out any negativity that you have in your spirit; negativity that has been sown by the words of other people and has had an effect on your life, weed it out and put it in the compost bin. Negativity that is the fruit of seeds that have taken root in your life and that you are now passing on to others, again get rid of it from the roots and cast it away from you forever. And having cleared the weeds, sow the seeds of positivity. Allow positivity to take root in your being, and let it grow so that it bears fruit and you can share it with those who come into contact with you.

As I was writing this chapter I received two SMS messages from younger members of my family. I had not realised but this was the day that young teens were getting the results of their GCSE examinations in England and Wales. The first message carried the news that the sender had done extremely well with a number of A stars, As and a B. The second message, again carried news of good results, but the sender was disappointed because her grades were not as good as her cousin's. Later that same day I heard of another young girl who had arrived at her part-time summer job in tears and very upset after receiving her own results that morning. This goes to reinforce my view that our system of exams only helps to emphasise the differences and make one person feel a failure against another's success. Should we really be putting our children under such pressure?

8

LIVING IN ABUNDANCE

I first came across the concept of *"Living In Abundance"* many years ago when a group of spiritual teachers and *"prophets"* were sharing their belief that it was never intended that we should live in a position of lack. Their view that god/the divine/the universal source had provided everything that we need so that we should be lacking in nothing, came as one of those light-bulb moments for me. It made sense to me, but it certainly wasn't something that I was able to bring into realisation overnight.

I fully embraced the idea of living in abundant health and made up my mind that I would not entertain the thought of being ill. You see, the fact is, we only ever have that which we receive. If we are to experience a life of abundance, we need to receive that abundance.

Okay, first of all we need to decide what we actually mean by the word *"abundance"*. The Latin word *"abuntantia"*, from which our English word comes, means *"overflowing"*. To live in abundance, therefore, means to overflow. The most important thing to see here is that in order to live in abundance we must not put a lid on what we have, we must let it overflow.

Now, I'm not just talking about material things when I look at abundance, I'm talking about life, and everything that is part of life. I'm talking about the physical/material, I'm talking about the emotional, I'm talking about the spiritual. Money, possessions, compassion, knowledge, wisdom, insight, inspiration, positive energy, peace, support; all these things are part of the positive aspects of life, and as such are things to be shared and to be allowed to run freely – to overflow. You know that you have an abundance of something when somebody says *"thank you"*, and you hadn't even realised that you had shared something with them.

The River Jordan flows into the Sea of Galilee, an expanse of water that is rich in life. There is an abundance of fish in the Sea of Galilee, all manner of aquatic life can be found there and local fishermen make their living from the fish they catch in its waters. At the southerly point of the Sea of Galilee, the River Jordan continues its journey out of the sea and down toward the Dead Sea. The Sea of Galilee and the Dead Sea are connected by the same Jordan River and yet, whereas in the north the Sea of Galilee is full of life, the Dead Sea has no life in it. No fish live in the dead sea, the waters there are unable to sustain any life. Just a comparatively short distance and connected by one river, yet such a different environment. Why?

If you take a look at a map of the area, you will see the River Jordan flowing into the Sea of Galilee at the northerly end and flowing out again at the southerly point. This constant flowing in, through and out again is the reason for the abundance of life to be found in the sea. Move southwards down the map and you will see the river flow into the

Dead Sea but there is no outlet for the water to flow out again, the result is that the water does not host life because there is no flow. The only way for the water to leave the Dead Sea is through evaporation. The excess, rather than flowing out and bringing life to other areas, simply evaporates and turns to mist and cloud. Of course, this mist and cloud is not wasted as it will go on to join other particles and form rain clouds, eventually bringing benefit to other places, but the sea itself remains dead and lifeless.

In order for us to know abundance we must both allow a flow into our lives and also a flow out of our lives. If nothing flows out, then there is no space to receive more. Our lives become lifeless, stale and stagnant – unable to nourish and provide life.

We must be prepared to allow what we have to overflow, to keep moving so that others benefit and, as a direct result, we too will benefit. This is true abundance.

Be still. Consider your life. Do you allow things to flow through you? Whether it is material things, spiritual things, intellectual things – do you hoard and hold on to what you have received in life or do you share it with those around you? Your knowledge, your wisdom, your riches, no matter how small or great, these things are not there for you alone, but for you to share for the greater good.

9

THE LAW OF ATTRACTION

There are so many books, CDs, DVDs, articles, and lectures about the Law of Attraction these days that it is hard to imagine that anyone with an interest in Holistic/Spiritual matters is unaware of what it is all about. Yet, we only have to look around our circle of friends and acquaintances to see that it is one thing to know about it, but an entirely different thing to actually live in the reality of it. So why is this?

Let me make it clear that I am a firm believer in the Law of Attraction, having witnessed and experienced it many times in my own life. However, having read many books on the subject and listened to the talks and watched the videos, it seems to me that it is often made to sound too easy, and is therefore misleading. First of all I would have to say that it is not as simple as asking for whatever you want and it will automatically come to you. Just because I really want something and have gone through all the steps of asking, visualising and thanking, does not mean that I will necessarily receive what I want.

Imagine two football teams playing each other in the cup final, both the coaches have read "*The Secret*" and really believe that by putting out the desire for their team to win the cup, the Law of

Attraction will bring that cup to them. That is just not going to happen. No matter how much they ask, believe, give thanks, visualise or sacrifice lambs, one of them is going to be disappointed. And for those of you who think a draw would be an answer, this is a cup final – it can't happen, there has to be a winner and a loser and the cup can only go back to one of the clubs.

Let's look at another scenario. Two women have both been to hear a prominent speaker talking about manifesting your desires. They both *"fall in love"* with the handsome speaker. Both of them, having listened to his teachings and being totally independent of the other, put out the desire that by a certain date six months in the future, this man would be their husband. It ain't gonna happen! They can both believe and do all the right things but they can't both marry him on the same day and live happily ever after. The fact that he is already married could be another slight stumbling block here.

So what am I saying? Is it all a load of rubbish or is there a way to see the Law of Attraction work in your life?

The good news is that it can and will work when certain things are in place, and the two most important things in my view are. a connection to spirit and a cleansing of the subconscious.

You may have often heard that once you have set your desire you must synchronise your vibrational frequency with the manifestation of what you want and with the source energy (you may call this: god, spirit, source, universe or whichever name you choose). I'm going to tell you now that, that method is a bit like putting the cart before the horse. The first and, in my opinion, the most important factor in realising your desires, is to make sure that your desires are in tune with the source energy. Take time to align your vibration with that of the universe, get in tune with what is right for you and for the higher good of all. The Law of Attraction has nothing to do with greed or "*laying up treasures on earth*", it is about bringing harmony, unity, blessing to all. Each one of us comes from spirit and we are all actually part of that same life-giving creative spirit, so when we are in tune with spirit, the things that we desire are not simply for ourselves but for the universe as a whole.

That may all sound rather grand and somewhat daunting so how can we get ourselves into alignment with the source energy? How do we put ourselves in a position where we are in tune and at one with the universe? How do we reach the mountain top and find ourselves in that place where we are once again connected with the source? Well, as big as that mountain might seem, the answer to how to get there is really quite simple and has been known to virtually every spiritual tradition, prophet, teacher and guru throughout history. Yes, it's those two words again – **Be Still**.

Take time each day to get away from the mundane, the material, the pressures and stress, the everyday activities and **Be Still**. It is in the stillness, in the quiet, in that state of meditation and contemplation that we can reconnect with that source energy of which we are a part. Yes, it takes discipline, it takes an act of will to set aside time each day to just be. Time to listen and learn from the spirit that is in us. The more time we spend in silence and stillness, the deeper into our self we can go and the stronger that connection with the source will be. This is when we know that our desires are the right desires, that our goals are the right goals, that we are not being driven by ego but by inspiration and truth. This is when we will see the Law of Attraction in action, manifesting our dreams and desires.

The second thing I want to look at here is the cleansing of our subconscious. When we took on this incarnation as a human being we subjected ourselves to the teachings and messages of other human beings. Each one of us, as we were growing up, was told a version of what was right and what was wrong. Our parents, teachers, siblings, friends, employers, spiritual leaders have all, over the years, said many things that have been swallowed up by our subconscious minds and are now stored in the memory on our "hard-drive"; always there, always reminding us even when we are not aware of it. Times when we were told, *"you'll never be any good at that"*, *"you'll never make anything good of your life"*, *"he will always be better than you"*, *"you're a failure"*, *"you'll never be rich"*, *"you'll end up in a dead-end job"*, so many negative seeds that have been sown in so many lives.

The problem with all these negative seeds taking root in our subconscious, is that no matter how positive the words and thoughts we project, if in the depths of our being we are still hearing the negativity of many years, and that little voice is still saying "you'll never make it", we will be unable to tune into the frequency of source and receive what can be ours. So, once again we ask, *"how can I clean out the subconscious of all this negativity?"* And once again the answer is amazingly simple. It is in fact the same answer – **Be Still**.

Using meditation and affirmation together, or self-hypnosis, or, if you feel you need help, the services of a hypnotherapist, counsellor or other practitioner to help clear away the negativity, you can bring yourself to the position of being able to tune into the frequency of source. Think of yourself as a two-way radio if you like. By tuning into the right frequency you will receive the message enabling you to know what to ask for. You can then send the message, asking for it to be given to you, and then you will be able to receive the manifestation of your desire.

Be Still and know, then you can ask and then you shall receive.

10
WHY MEDITATE?

Don't meditate because you feel you should or because you feel you must, as if it is a duty or a condition in order to attain enlightenment. This is bondage and will not lead to life.

Meditate because you know that it is right and good.

But what do we mean by meditation? There are many different types and methods of meditation that one can explore and practice. Some involve the chanting of mantras, some involve assuming specific body positions, some involve total silence. Some forms of meditation are linked to a particular spiritual path whilst others have no association with any religious teaching.

When I talk about meditation, whatever method I might be using, the key words have to be, awareness, mindfulness or consciousness. Meditation is not about having a blank mind, it's not about clearing your mind of all thoughts, it is about being in control of your thoughts. Meditation is about being aware; aware of where you are, aware of who you are.

A simple method to aid you in your first steps on the meditation journey is to be aware of your breathing. Breathing is something we all do, all the time. As you sit reading this book you are continuing to breathe. You were breathing when you got up this morning, you were breathing when you went to bed last night. In fact you have been breathing since the moment the midwife brought you into the world and you took your first breath. You've not had to think about it or make yourself do it; you have just continued to do it throughout your life. But, as you start to meditate, I actually want you to think about your breathing and to concentrate on it, so find yourself somewhere comfortable to sit down and we will start the meditation process.

Close your eyes and take a deep breath in, directing your mind to a place just below your nose as you allow the air to flow into your nostrils and down into your lungs. Next, I want you to slowly release that air in a nice, slow stream, once again concentrating on that space below your nose or in front of your mouth. Keep breathing out until all the air has been expelled from your lungs. Now continue this process repeatedly, all the time being aware of your breathing and concentrating on the act of inhaling and exhaling. Be aware of how you feel as you breathe deeply. You will probably discover that your breath out will take about twice the time that you take to breathe in, maybe even longer. How does this feel as you empty your lungs? Just concentrate on your breathing, continuing to breathe in and out at a nice, slow rhythm. You will probably also notice that your mind and your thoughts start wandering off in all directions, thinking about things that have happened during the day, things that are going to happen tomorrow, what you are going to have for dinner tonight. None of this matters, it is perfectly natural for you to have these thoughts come into your head, don't try to fight them and don't try to ignore them – they are there, so acknowledge them and put them aside. When these thoughts do start to crowd in simply take your awareness back to your breathing. Speak to yourself "breathe in, breathe out". Believe me, when you are concentrating on your breathing it actually becomes very difficult to think about anything else. Just allow yourself to stay in the "now" and connect with each breath.

Where you go from here is entirely up to you. There are so many different methods and techniques linked to meditation, the important thing is to find what works for you. My own personal preference is to journey inside myself and spend time in that quiet, calm, peaceful place, which is at the centre of our being. It is my belief and experience that all the answers we need to any problem or question, can be found within us, rather than anywhere outside us. By meditating, we can connect with that inner spirit, which is part of the source spirit, the creative energy of the universe, which is very much a part of each one of us, and we are very much a part of the whole of that energy.

So, getting back to the question at the beginning of this chapter, Why Meditate? Meditate in order realise your connection to the universal life force, the divine mind, the source energy of all energy, god. And when we are aware of that connection we can know all there is to know. Take time each day to **Be Still** and know.

11
ONENESS

There are no spirits – just Spirit.

There are no gods – just God.

Spirit, God, Source, Life Energy, Universe, The Divine Mind – All is one.

All is one.

We are one.

We began as Spirit.

We continue as Spirit.

Spirit is life.

Life is energy.

Energy has no end.

We have no end.

We are one.

12
RESPONSIBILITY

This may come as a surprise to some readers but:

You are responsible for your own thoughts, your own actions, your own words, in fact you are responsible for your own life. You can't blame anyone else for things that happen in your life, you can't even give anyone else the credit for how your life is and how you live your life. It is your responsibility as to how you react to others and for the decisions you make based on the influence of others.

At a recent workshop, where the facilitator had been talking about the Law of Attraction, one participant said that she believed our whole lives were mapped out and planned for us, before we even appeared in this incarnation. She believed that the reason everything always went wrong for her was because that was the way it was meant to be, and she could not change that. *"No matter how well I live my life, other people always throw it back in my face and trample me down"*. I'm sad to say that if that is the way she believes it will be, then that is the way it will be. That is the Law of Attraction in action.

The one who thinks negativity will attract negativity. That is our own responsibility. We choose to accommodate the thoughts that hang around in our minds, nobody forces us to hang on to these thought patterns, these thought habits; it is purely our own responsibility as to what we allow ourselves to dwell on.

Every thought that I have is my own, I am responsible for what I think. All of my thoughts come from within me and it is up to me whether I dwell on those thoughts or dismiss them from my mind. Admittedly, many thoughts are brought on by external influences; I may see something as I am walking down the road that stirs up a thought in me, I may hear something on the radio, or something that somebody says that causes a thought to rise to the surface, but if that thought is a negative, or harmful thought, then it is my responsibility to acknowledge that thought, take hold of it and discard it.

Be still. Imagine that you are sitting at the computer, create a new folder on your desktop and label it negativity. Now right click on the folder's icon and select the option "*delete*". Once you click on "*delete*" a warning window appears asking if you are sure that you want to permanently delete negativity – answer yes and click on the button.

It is not just the negative things that we are responsible for, it is every thought and action, every word that we speak. It never ceases to amaze me how many people who claim to be "spiritual" hide behind their so-called spirituality, refusing to take responsibility for the things they say or do. Phrases such as "my *spirit guide told me* . . . . .", "*It was channelled through me by* . . . . . .", "*they told me* . . . . .", often make me shudder. What they really mean is "*I think* . . . .", "*I had this idea* . . ."

I can't begin to tell you the number of times that a medium has come up to me, uninvited, to tell me that they have a message from a relative for me. The relative is described, names given, characteristics about them and I have absolutely no idea who they are talking about. The descriptions bear no resemblance to anyone that I have ever known, yet the medium insists that he/she must be right because that is what they are being told.

I'm not saying that all mediums are deluded, or are frauds, I understand that, for some people, mediums and mediumship can bring a lot of help and comfort. I do admit that I have difficulty in accepting that the individual spirits of those departed return to give what are usually very trivial, or vague, messages to their loved ones. The whole idea doesn't really fit into my belief that we are all one and part of the same divine spirit, but I am open to receive any evidence to the contrary.

What concerns me is their dogmatic belief that they are right, and that the voices they hear are what they believe they are. How many horrendous crimes have been committed by people who have been told to do so by the voices in their heads?

Intuition is a fantastic thing, and can be used to help so many people if used correctly, but accept it for what it is - intuition. Take responsibility. If you are sensing things that you should convey to others, then learn to develop this ability and accept that it is coming from within you, from that place inside you that is aligned to spirit, and take responsibility for how you share it. And if you happen to be wrong, face up to it; don't hide behind *"the spirits told me, so it must be right"*.

The other concern I have with regard to responsibility, is the growing number of books and articles claiming to have been channelled by "*ascended masters*" or other spiritual beings. One would expect these books to produce some amazing revelatory teachings, but very often they provide us with nothing new, and are often not very exciting or earth shattering.

I have recently had dealings with someone who is not backward in coming forward to declare that they have been chosen to channel the "*Christ consciousness, Muhammad, the Buddha, the Virgin Mary and countless other sainted beings*". At the same time this person has been waging a personal battle on the internet with accusations and counter accusations regarding something which, true or not, would have been better dealt with in private between the parties concerned. *"By their fruits shall you know them."*

I feel that I should point out here that everything I am writing comes from me and is not channelled by any external being. These are my thoughts and my opinions. I would like to think that I am writing from a place of connection, of oneness with the creative energy, but that is my responsibility. The key here is to formulate these thoughts and opinions by being still and going deep within, to the divine source that is within every one of us. We need to acknowledge our own responsibility for the things we say and do and recognise that at times we may not be 100% right.

Be still. Are the thoughts and opinions we hold really coming from that still space deep inside, or are they being influenced by outside forces or even by ego? Examine the purity of motive in what you say, are you out to impress? To make a name for yourself? To show how "*spiritual*" you are in the hope that people will take more notice of what you say, because you have been chosen as a channel by some mysterious ascended master or spiritual being? May all that we say or do, come from a place of stillness and purity with no ulterior motive.

13

WORSHIP

Spirit does not require worship, only respect.

A genuinely enlightened being, whether Jesus, Mohammed, Buddha, Krishna, or any other avatar does not demand worship.

Worship is a thing of ego, not of enlightenment.

Worship is a thing of fear and is linked with the human motive of *"power over"*.

If any man says, *"worship me"*, or *"worship this god or that god"*, do not listen.

We are all spirit. I am spirit, you are spirit. There is no difference. If we worship spirit (source, god, universe etc.) we are only worshipping ourselves. This is ego.

Be still. Know that you are connected to the divine source, to spirit. Know that all are connected to the divine source, to spirit. Respect yourself and respect all. This, not worship, is your calling.

14

THE PUZZLE

There was once a prominent inspirational writer who had a very important article to write for an international magazine. He was working very hard to meet the deadline but was struggling a little because of a series of distractions. The writer's wife was out at work while he was battling with the laptop and it was the middle of the school holidays, so he was also having to watch out for his 6-year old son who was at home.

On this particular day it was raining very heavily and so the boy was unable to go and play in the garden. As the day went on the boy was getting more and more bored in the house and kept going into his father's study, asking questions and wanting attention. The father was finding it increasingly difficult to give his attention to his work and also, at the same time, to his son. Trying to find something to keep his son occupied he was looking through a pile of papers on his desk and came across a map of the world in one of the magazines. The answer to his problem.

The father took a pair of scissors and proceeded to cut the picture of the map into small, jigsaw-like, pieces. He then handed all the pieces to his son and sent him into another room and told him to put the pieces back together and when he had finished putting the world back together he could then come and show him.

"This should keep the boy quiet for an hour or so", he thought, and went back to working on his article.

After only 10 minutes, the young boy appeared in the doorway of the study, holding a board with the completed and restored map of the world. The father was amazed.

"How on earth did you manage to finish it so quickly", said the father.

"Well, it was easy really," replied the boy, *"I noticed that on the back of the map was a picture of a man and I thought that, if I could get the man right, then the world would fall into place"*.

Be still. We spend so much time looking at the world and wanting to change it, getting frustrated or angry with the way things are, when really we should be looking at ourselves to see those same things in us that are not right and need changing. As we get our own lives in order, so the world around us will start to show order. If we each sort out our own failings and faults, then the immediate world around will fall into place, and eventually the whole world will fall into place.

15

FLY LIKE AN EAGLE

Since the first human stepped out of his cave into the sunlight and looked around and above him at the wonders of creation, the beautiful, graceful and magical movement of the birds of the air has been a fascination. We have stood in the forest clearing and on the cliff tops and wondered at the freedom of flight, puzzling and longing to be able to take to the air.

Over the years we have made all sorts of contraptions to try to get us airborne, jumped off cliffs, strapped feathers and materials to us, developed mechanical devices in order to conquer the mystery of flight. The challenge of flight has captured the imagination and indeed, it is only in relatively recent years that we have discovered ways to reach the skies. This longing to fly has been symbolic of our longing to rise above the natural limitations of mortality and to soar into the realm of the supernatural. This yearning to fly, to rise above, is not simply a physical desire but is also a spiritual one, and the universe has made provision for us to have all our spiritual needs met. So why is it then that so few of us manage to actually soar up high on a spiritual level? How can we free ourselves from the limitations of our human existence and fly into the realm of the supernatural?

As I look at the wonders of creation, and as I get older, I become more and more aware that nothing is an accident. Everything that is, is there for a reason. There, so that we can learn something from it. I'm a long way from learning all those lessons and an even longer way from knowing what the reasons are for everything that is, but I am learning and moving forward.

One part of creation that I have been aware of for many years, and its lesson for us, is the wonderful, majestic eagle. A favourite book of mine which I have read many times over the years is William Horwood's "*Stonor Eagles*". The book creates a parallel between the life of a sea eagle and that of a human as their separate journeys link together in a wonderful spiritual adventure. Many years before that, I was blessed to hear Ern Baxter, whom many regarded as a 20th Century prophet and teacher, speaking about life on eagles' wings, where he described the life of the eagle as a spiritual allegory. Although the path that Ern Baxter took was not the path for me, I have never forgotten his words, and much of what I write in this chapter is inspired by what I heard him say back then in 1976/77.

The Old Testament prophet, Isaiah, said *"They that wait upon the Lord shall renew their strength; they shall mount up with wings as eagles"*

What does that mean? It means exactly what it says. The key word here is *"Wait"*, it simply means to spend time to meditate, meditate on the divine, spirit, universe, god, source, whatever you want to call it, and you will become strong again and rise up as an eagle rises up, high into the sky, soaring above the earth and the earthly, and reaching up into spiritual realms.

Now, I know that not everybody finds it easy to meditate, to still their mind and control their thoughts. I've even heard the Dalai Lama confess to having difficulty in disciplining himself to meditate, so there is no shame in not being an expert. So let's turn the rest of this piece into a guide for a meditation on the magic of the eagle's flight. Once you have read it and read it again, take time out to really consider the eagle, how it lives and how it flies. Let the words sink in and become a part of you.

Just as we consider the lion to be the king of the jungle, so we often describe the eagle as being the king of the birds. The eagle has come to represent strength and beauty, freedom, regality and splendour. As we all come from the same Source, we too have the potential of soaring into divine realms.

I've decided to use various quotations from the bible in order to illustrate the life of the eagle, not because I am a follower of Christianity or Judaism, but because the bible does seem to have a lot to say about eagles and these words can be of particular benefit to us as we meditate on the dharma of the eagle. It is also worth pointing out here that in that part of the world where the bible originated there are two types of eagle, the Golden Eagle and the Imperial Eagle and much of what we will look at here relates to these two types of bird.

The old testament book of Deuteronomy has these words: *"As an eagle stirs up her nest, fluttering over her young, spreading her wings, she takes them and bears them on her wings"*.

I don't know if you have ever watched a wildlife programme about eagles, or seen photographs of young eaglets – let's face it, a young eaglet is a long way from the majestic adult who soars the skies. Squalling and weird-looking, this little creature needs to learn how to fly if it is going to reach the heights that it is destined for.

As this young bird sits in the nest, its mother flies back and forth bringing it food each day to satisfy its ravenous appetite. What a fantastic life, all it has to do is sit there in the nest while its mother brings the food. It doesn't have to do a thing, not even chew the food as it is dropped straight into its mouth. It's a bit like us as we start off on our spiritual journey. All we need to do is read the books, listen to the CDs, go to conferences and be fed by the "experts", the experienced ones. We just open our mouths and let them feed us. It couldn't be any better. We are so impressed by the powerful knowledge of the teachers, the gurus, the spiritual leaders and inspirational speakers.

Likewise, the young eagle cannot but be impressed by the powerful wings of the parent. But alongside its power and majesty is a gentle side as she sits on the nest and the eaglet snuggles in securely underneath the warmth and softness of those great wings. In the same way we can feel secure surrounded by the knowledge and experience of those who have trodden the path before us.

All is well in the nest, until one day the mother starts to act in a rather curious manner. Instead of landing on the nest she begins to hover, beating the air with her wings. She then begins to take a bit of the nest in her beak and drop it to the ground. She follows this by taking another peck of the nest and discarding it toward the ground below.

I can imagine that this might be a bit scary for the eaglet, as it begins to think that maybe its mother has started to lose it! With each tug of the beak, the nest is becoming smaller and smaller and the safety of the eaglet is diminishing with it. As the nest continues to disappear, the eaglet begins to realise that the comfort and security it had relied on, is no longer there to support it. And so, the eagle flight-training programme begins.

When we come into this world in the present incarnation we have chosen, we first need to spend time as children, being nurtured, nourished and protected, but pretty soon the universe, or source of our being, will begin to confront us with the need to grow and to mature into more than the earth-bound creatures that we begin our lives as.

It is important to note here that the one who is causing the seeming problem to the young eaglets in the nest, is the one who has most concern for their well-being, the one who has the most love for them. We often blame god or fate or the universe when things get a little uncomfortable in our lives and things seem to be going wrong, but what if we view these situations in a different light? What if we see that this is the universe's way of stirring the nest and encouraging us to rise above and to reach new heights?

As the nest slowly disappears and the young eaglet is now standing on the ledge of what is left of its home, the mother bird then takes the eaglet in her beak and "*encourages*" him to the edge. It is probably at this point that the offspring starts to have serious doubts about the sanity of its parent. Next, mother pushes the young bird over the edge and it falls headlong towards the ground and certain destruction. Suddenly, as if from nowhere, mother swoops beneath the youngster, catching it on her back and flies with it back to the nest and to safety.

The young eaglet is just getting over this traumatic experience, when it starts all over again. Mother bird, once again starts to nudge her young and once again he falls towards the ground, only to be rescued on the back of his mother just before impact. This whole process is repeated several times, each time the parent catches the youngster before tragedy occurs. After being convinced of the insanity of its parent, the young eaglet starts to wonder if mum is actually trying to get some message across to him here! Thinking about the powerful wings that carry mother and baby back up to the relative safety of the nest, he begins to think that maybe he should try doing something with his own wings. So the next time he feels himself falling from a great height, he very shakily starts to spread his wings and, to his amazement, finds himself rising up, higher and higher as the air currents carry him far above the nest that had been his safety and security for all of his life. He is no longer a chick, begging for food that his mother brings to him, rather he is now learning to become a mature eagle, king of the birds of the air.

Just like that young eagle being nudged out of the safety of its nest, we can turn circumstances that might scare us and make us feel insecure into launching pads, so that we can soar up high and rise above every circumstance.

The Book of Proverbs describes *"the mystery of an eagle in the air"* as "one of the mysteries of the universe that is too hard to understand."

The eagle can fly higher than any other bird without ever having to flap its wings. Earlier I spoke about *"mounting up as eagles"*; this description gives us a picture of ease, of soaring high and free. There is no image of an eagle flapping, an eagle doesn't flap, it soars effortlessly on the currents; perching on the edge of a cliff, waiting for the right wind, and when it comes the eagle will launch into the air, reaching high into the sky. Again, the secret here is waiting. Being still and knowing. Not getting *"into a flap"*, but being conscious of how the wind is blowing and allowing the current to take it and carry it.

Not only does the eagle know the secret of effortless flight, it also reaches heights higher than any other bird can fly; allowing the currents to take it higher than the squawking of other birds, higher than any possible distractions. It reaches a height that allows it to see far more and to have a clearer picture from such a vantage. There is no way we can actually know what the world looks like to the eagle, but we can be sure from studying the anatomy of their eyes, that they must be able to see a greatly magnified and more enlarged view than we could see with our eyes. A human has 200,000 cone cells per millimetre, that send light information to the brain, whereas the eagle has around 1,000,000 cone cells per millimetre, making their vision not only greater but far clearer than our own.

By watching and waiting, by being still and sensitive to the spiritual currents, we too can *"mount up with wings as eagles"*, allowing us to rise above the mundane and to have a clearer and wider vision. As spiritual beings it is not our calling to be crawling on the ground, or even sitting on telegraph poles, but to be flying above into higher realms.

So, what are our limits? How high can we fly? We all come from the same source, the same divine imagination that created and creates. Whether you want to call this source *"god"* or *"spirit"*, *"universe"* or *"the divine creator"*, it doesn't matter. Whatever you call it, this source is limitless, is not bound by physical or material restraints; and what the source can do – you can do. I'll say it once again, you were made to rise above all the physical and material limitations that you have come to believe are real – they are not real, they are simply an illusion. There are no limitations other than those we create in our minds – spirit is without limits. All you need to do is to be still and wait, be aware of your connection with the source-energy and allow the spirit in you to rise up and fly. The divine nature that we came from is ours. You don't need to look outside of yourself for god; all that you need is within you and is you.

One final thing to observe about the eagle is that it never panics. Even when it gets sick or is dying, it will sit on a rock allowing the healing power of the sun to work. The eagle waits. The eagle is still. When the eagle knows that its time in this life is coming to an end, it finds a place on a high rock, watches the sun and waits.

Be still. As you wait, and observe, you will know when the time is right, when the current is right to carry you. By rushing headlong you will only fall. Be still, be quiet, watch and listen. Be aware and trust your source.

16
FAITH

We often hear people saying things such as, *"My faith has carried me through"*, *"If it wasn't for my faith, I could not have endured this"*, *"He was a man of great faith"*. But what, exactly, is faith? Is it real? Is it just some sort of misguided hope? Is it really necessary? And if so, what should we have faith in?

The Oxford English Dictionary defines faith as

> *"Complete trust or confidence in someone or something"*

The bible, in the book of Hebrews, says this about faith:

> *"Faith is the substance of things hoped for, the evidence of things unseen"*

So then, it would seem that faith is not just a blind belief in something that we hope might happen. It's not about enduring the problems of life because everything is going to be ok in the next life or in heaven. Faith is not about *"pie in the sky when you die"*, rather it is about manifestation. It is about the realisation of those thoughts, aspirations and inspirations that come from the spirit within.

Faith is often confused with belief, whereas in fact (in my belief) they are two separate things, even though there are certain crossovers between the two, in the same way that both a daffodil and an orchid are flowers but, at the same time, are also very different.

I've never been there, but I believe that there is a place somewhere in the world called the Tubai Islands, somewhere in the South Pacific. I doubt very much that I will ever visit there and see them for myself, but I still believe that they are there.

Faith, though, is about seeing or realising that which we have believed.

If I have faith that if I lay my hands on someone who is ill they will be healed, that faith is rewarded with evidence and the person is healed.

For me, the most important application of faith is to know that by living and walking in spirit, my life will see a manifestation of abundance, the fullness of life. I don't need to worry or stress about my life, I just need to live it, to be.

Be still. Take time to consider where your life is. Are you trusting in your own efforts? Are you trusting in the material world? Or do you have faith that your source will take care of all the things that you need to make your life fulfilled.

17

CLEARING SPACE

Do you want more?

What do you want more of?

Money? Time? Love? Things?

Does your desire for more mean that you are protective and possessive about what you already have?

You feel you don't have enough money and want to have more, so you hold on tightly to what you already have.

You want more time to be able to do things, so you guard your time carefully and ration your use of the time that you do have.

You feel that you want to attract love, yet you are reluctant to give love especially to yourself.

Whatever it is you feel that you want more of, does it make you hold on more tightly to what you already have?

Picture, if you will, a bookcase, cram-packed with books next to each other, on top of each other, scattered on the floor around the bookcase. Books that you have never actually looked at for years, books that somebody bought for you as a present, but you are never really likely to read, books that you enjoyed reading, books that you didn't really get into, so many books. You'd like to go out and buy some new books that you particularly want to read, but you know that you no longer have any space left where you can put the books. But you really want these new books. What do you do?

The answer, as is so often the case, is simple. First of all, you have a clear out. You get rid of all the books that you are never likely to read, all the ones that you might have read before but have sat on the bookshelves for months, maybe years, without their pages being turned. It doesn't matter what you do with them, pass them on to friends, sell them at a car-boot sale, donate them to a charity shop – just clear them out and make space for those new ones that need to come into your life.

No rocket science there, and the same principle applies to all the other things that you want or that you feel are missing from your life. Yes, this works on the spiritual, emotional and material planes. Whatever it is that you want more of, you must first be prepared to let go and give away what you already have.

Not enough Space.

Your feel that your house is too small, you need more space so you want to move to somewhere bigger, but at the moment you don't think you can afford it? Ok, first off, do some clearing out – make some space and then watch the changes happen. Get rid of EVERYTHING that you don't need or use. I have heard it said that if you have something that you haven't looked at, worn or used in the last 6 months you should seriously think about getting rid of it. If you have something that you haven't looked at, worn or used in the last 12 months, you should definitely get rid of it. Books, gadgets, clothes, CDs, all those boxes of stuff that are stored in the cupboard under the stairs – you've managed without them for a whole year now – You don't need them – Get rid of them. As you de-clutter and make space, you will be amazed at how things change. You will find more peace, you will be calmer, have less stress and see things change. Maybe you will even find that you have the resources to find that bigger house as the universe acknowledges the fact that you are doing your bit to clear space.

Not enough Money.

Most of us at some point in our lives have found ourselves in a situation when we think we need more money, whether it is to buy something we have set our sights on, or simply to pay our bills. Each month the bills seem to be getting higher and increasing at a greater rate than the amount coming in. So we rely on the little plastic card and then find that, as a result, the following month the bills are even higher.

Now, this may be a bit harder to understand and to put into practice, but exactly the same principle applies here as it does to creating space. It took me a long time to get to grips with this, and even now I have to be honest and admit that there are times when I get thoughts in my head telling me that this is insane, and I have to remind myself that it is not the thoughts in my head that I should listen to but the voice in my inner spirit.

Remember the reference to the Sea of Galilee in chapter 8? We need to allow things to flow through us in order for them to keep coming in. This is all about living in the now and not thinking of the future, or even the past. So, consider the situation, it is Tuesday and you have £50 in your pocket, in fact that is all the money you have. You know that on the following Monday you need to pay a particular bill of £85 and you don't really know where the money is going to come from in time to meet the deadline, but it is still only Tuesday. Later that day, you find yourself in a situation where a colleague at work, or a friend or family member comes to you in desperation. They tell you that, for whatever reason, they need to borrow £30 – it is a serious situation and they really need that money, maybe to travel to a job interview or to visit someone in hospital. Whatever it is, their need is genuine, but they also tell you that they wouldn't be able to pay you back until next month.

Step back for a minute and look at the situation. They need the money today, you have that money today. You don't need the money until next Monday, anything can happen between now and then, you have no way of knowing. Right now it is Tuesday and there is a need today that you can meet.

You offer to give the £30 in the knowledge that you don't actually need it today. You are able to be used as an instrument of the universe in providing for the needs of another, and so you trust the universe to provide for your needs when the time arrives. The following morning comes along and the postman brings you a letter from the Inland Revenue with an unexpected tax-rebate and a cheque for £150. Not only is it enough to pay your bill, which, if you deposit the cheque in your bank today, will have cleared by Monday when you need to pay your bill, but there is extra – an abundance. This sort of attitude needs faith, faith in the universe that you are part of and one with. As you are used by the universe to meet the needs of others, so others will be used by the universe to meet your needs when they arise.

Another word for money is currency, currency is energy, flowing energy. Money is energy that needs to keep flowing. In the situation described, if you had decided that you couldn't help your friend because you would need the money yourself at a time in the future, there is a very strong chance that when your own bill arrived that you would still have your £50 but would be £35 short of the £85 that you needed.

Just one more important note while we are talking about money. In the above scenario, your motive and intention needs to be pure and right. Don't help somebody else simply because you think by doing so that you will benefit. Don't think about tomorrow; help because you care, because you have compassion, because it is the right thing to do.

Not enough Time.

One of the battles I have fought for many years is with regard to time-management. I've always had problems, believing that I did not have enough time to do all the many things that needed to be done. This would usually cause me to stress and, as a result I would find that I then had even less time available to me. This was another lesson that has taken me quite a while to grasp. The first thing to realise is that time is only a concept that we use to help us measure the days. As we talked about in Chapter 3, there is only one time, and that time is Now. If we can come to a true and practical understanding of this, we will also come to a realisation that time is not important. We only actually have this moment so we use this moment in the most beneficial and productive way possible. Don't waste time, this moment, by thinking about what has gone before and, perhaps more importantly, don't waste time, this moment, by thinking about what might be in the future.

In a similar way to the other examples in this chapter, if you really feel that you need more time, you first need to give up some time. Whether that is giving time to others who will benefit from your time, or whether it means re-arranging your time, so that you are giving up the time that you spend on unimportant things and activities, doesn't really matter. The important thing is realising that the only time that you have is now, and so you have a responsibility to use that time wisely and in the best possible way.

Not enough Love.

One thing I hear too often, is people desperately looking for love, for a relationship, or for a soul mate. And what happens, more often than not, is that they spend so much time looking for Mr or Miss Right, that they never actually realise that what they are looking for is right in front of them. To receive love, you have to give love. I'm not talking about spreading your love around in some needy way, what I'm really saying is that firstly you need to give some love to yourself. If you can't love yourself, you can't expect someone else to love you. If you can't love yourself, you can never really love someone else in a real, unconditional way. Give your love, firstly to your self, and as you give it away you will make room to receive love.

Be still. Spend some time thinking about what it is that you really want to bring into your life, and then look at how you can first give that away in order to clear space, to make room so that you can receive. Think about your breathing, breathe slowly and deeply, breathing in and out. Notice that the longer you exhale, the more fresh air you can inhale. As you empty your lungs of air, you can then fill them with fresh air. The more you give out, the more you are able to receive.

18

SEIZE THE DAY

When the day comes for me to leave this body and pass on to whatever comes next, I don't want people to have to say;

"He died too soon; he was still waiting for the right time to act on his dreams"

The old saying, *"don't put off until tomorrow what you can do today"*, is something that should be a mantra used every day when you wake up.

Today is the only day you have; there is only one time . . . . Now. You cannot be sure that tomorrow will come, so why even think about it?

Be Still Spend some time to think about all those things that you know would be right to do, but are always putting off. Make a list and then do them. Do them today, not tomorrow. Phone that family member or friend to tell them how you really feel about them, that you love them. Apologise to that person that you have upset or wronged, whether intentionally or not. Write your will; make sure that your house is in order so that others don't have added stress should you pass over unexpectedly. Sort out that holiday that you have been promising yourself. Act now while you have the ability and time.

19
PILLOW TALK

Some time ago, before Kiera and I opened up The Centre, I had just started renting a therapy room above an holistic shop, in order to have a base for my Sound Therapy treatments. I was driving in one morning thinking to myself, *"I must get a pillow today; I really have to get a pillow today."*

I had everything else sorted out in my room, all my equipment, Tibetan and Crystal Singing Bowls, Gongs, Drums, Tuning Forks etc, the treatment couch was set up, with blankets to keep the client warm, but I had forgotten to get a pillow, so I had been using folded up blankets to place under the client's head. I really needed to get a pillow.

I arrived at the centre and had barely had time to take my coat off and enjoy a cup of tea, when a man opened the front door. He was carrying a bundle under his arm and he asked me, *"You don't know anyone who might need a pillow do you?"*

I don't know if it is possible to be any more random than that. The timing was perfect, I needed a pillow and here was a complete stranger that I had never laid eyes on before and would probably never lay eyes on again, but who was trying to find someone to take the exact thing that I was wanting that day.

It has been said that *"you don't attract what you want, you attract what you are."* I guess that makes me a pillow in that case.

But being a pillow isn't as crazy as it might sound. A pillow gives comfort and rest, and if I attract that because that's what I am, then I am doing something right. If through my life I can offer comfort and rest, If I can bring peace and calm to those who lean on me, then I'm happy.

Be still. Take a look at your life and what it is that you continue to attract. Are you attracting problems into your life? Are you attracting want and need? Maybe you are attracting bad relationships. Look inside and ask yourself what it is that you need to change in order to attract love, abundance, peace, healing. You attract what you are, so be love, be support, be pure, be whole in your spirit and observe the changes that will occur in and around your life as you change from within, rather than trying to change things from without.

20

BUT I DON'T UNDERSTAND

I meet a lot of people who say to me, *"but I don't understand, how does it work? How does this whole 'spirituality' thing work?"*

Do you know what? It doesn't really matter how it works, and you don't have to understand it in order to experience it.

I'm writing this on my lap-top and I haven't got the faintest idea how computers work; the electric light is on – how all that energy travels across the country through strands of wires, I can't begin to explain. I was just talking to somebody on my cell phone, there are not even any wires there to carry the energy. And how on earth can I put a small round disc into a machine and then hear and watch people talking and moving. I'm just an ordinary person who has very little knowledge of technology, but even though I don't know *how* it works, I can still use it and enjoy the benefits of it. I flick the switch and the light comes on, I tap in some numbers and I can talk to somebody on the other side of the globe, I click the remote and sit back to enjoy a movie. I don't need to know how, I just let it happen.

Living an inspired life, a life *"in spirit"*, is not about understanding, it's not even about believing, it's about living in faith.

Be still. Don't waste time and energy trying to work out what it means to be living in spirit and enjoying a life of abundance. Just trust that if you find time to be still and silent, then the spirit that you are part of and connected to, the spirit that is inside you, will live through you. You are not a body that has a soul; you are a soul that has a body. You are spirit dwelling in a physical body. Allow spirit to live and to manifest through your material form.

21

RAINDROP MEDITATION

As with the earlier meditation in this book, you may find it useful to record these words and then play them back when you are ready to practise the meditation.

Find a space where you can be still without being disturbed. Sit down, or lie down in a comfortable position, making sure that you are not restricted in any way. Close your eyes and breathe slowly. Relax your whole body from the top of your head, right down to the soles of your feet. Continue to breathe slowly and as you breathe in, imagine that you are breathing in the positive energy of the universe. As you breathe out, you are breathing out all those things that you no longer want to hold on to in your life.

Now, as you relax, I want you to slowly count from 1 to 10, and as you do so, imagine that you are drifting away, up into the air, floating higher and higher 1 . . . . . 2 . . . . 3 . . . . 4 floating higher, 5 . . . . . . 6 . . . . . . 7 . . . . . higher and higher, 8 . . . . . 9 . . . . 10, until you find yourself entering into, and becoming one with, a beautiful cloud. And as you become one with this cloud, you are aware that you are floating gently through the sky. Floating through the sky you look down over the beautiful landscape below you, the trees and the hills, the rivers and the mountains.

Slowly you float, until you are hovering over the top of a very large hill and you are aware that you are transforming into a tiny droplet of water and the cloud gently releases the refreshing rain that it holds. You are now a drop of rain amongst the myriad of other drops of rain as you gently fall towards the earth.

As you touch the earth, you soak through the surface, going deeper and deeper until you join with and become one with other drops of rain in an underground stream. Still that drop of water, but now part of the stream, you flow with the stream until you emerge from the earth and through the rocks as part of a refreshing, freshwater spring. You are now part of the spring as it flows down the side of the hill until it joins even more water, and you are now part of a stream that flows even further down the hill. And as you flow with the stream, you are in total unity with all the other drops of water that make up this one moving stream.

Eventually, you join with even more water as many streams come together to form a flowing river. You are still that same drop of rain water, but now you have joined with and are one with many other drops in this growing and flowing river. Feel what it is like to be part of this river, the feeling of flowing, of running over rocks, of heading to a destination without having to think about where you are going, as the current of the river guides and carries you.

Now as you continue to flow with the river you are aware of more changes happening, the mass of water is now so much bigger. As the river flows into the sea, you are still that same drop of water but you are also part of and at one with the ocean. And as you are one with the ocean it is impossible to see yourself as that individual rain drop any longer. You are connected to the ocean which in turn is connected to every other ocean on the surface of the planet. You are one with, and the same as, that mass of water that covers the majority of the earth's surface.

You now continue to flow with the tides and you feel the incredible energy that you are not only a part of, but the energy that is, in fact, you. Enjoy that feeling, that energy, that power, that excitement that is you. Spend a little time now experiencing it.

After a while, you are aware of more changes taking place. As the sun shines down on the ocean, heating the water, you are aware of another sensation. You rise from the ocean as a particle of mist, rising up higher and higher until once again you become part of and one with a cloud, which floats through the air, over the sea and the land, and once again you see the landscape below you as you float over it, until you come to hover over the top of a hill, and once again the cycle continues as you gently fall to the earth as a drop of rain.

As you come to the end of this meditation, I want you to consider that, even though you have your own physical individuality, you are also part of and one with the energy of the universe. You are part of and one with the source of all things, god, spirit, the divine, the energy of life. Consider this and dwell on it for a moment before you become aware again of your body and your surroundings.

Finally, take two or three slow deep breaths, have a good stretch and open your eyes. Come back to the present and once again make contact with the earth.

*

We are all unique individuals in these human bodies that are home to our spirit, yet we are all one and the same spirit, interdependent, interconnected, and joined together as one.

22

TUNE IN

Do you sometimes find it hard to hear what spirit is saying, or to see which way spirit is guiding? Do you sometimes find it hard to know what it is that you are meant to be doing or what you need to be learning? Is it because god, or spirit, is not communicating with you?

Once again the answer is simple. You're not hearing or receiving from spirit because you are not tuned in. There is nothing complicated here, if your radio or TV is not switched on and tuned in to the correct frequency it does not mean that the station is not broadcasting. The radio waves are constantly travelling through the atmosphere, they don't just switch on when the receiver is switched on, they are always there.

I remember as a child we used to have a big old wireless set in the house. Long before digital or transistors we had to wait for the valves to warm up before the thing would work properly. I used to love turning the dial on the front of the set and listen to all the strange voices and music coming from inside the wireless. And all the wonderful names printed on the face as the needle moved along to the turning of the dial. Names like Hilversum, Luxembourg, Kalundborg, Motala, Ankara, Allouis, & Tromso. I would have great fun listening to the different languages coming from different parts of the world as all these radio waves were travelling through the atmosphere and I was able to catch them as the needle reached different spots as the dial turned. All I had to do was tune in to the right frequency to pick up the signal, whether it came from London, Dublin, or mainland Europe.

Spirit is communicating all the time, the only reason you are not getting the message is because you are not tuned in.

So what do we need to do in order to tune in?

Be still.

As you rest in that place of stillness which is spirit, imagine an antenna attached to your soul or, better still, imagine that you are the centre of a giant satellite dish. Adjust your tuning dial until you start to pick up the broadcast signal from the universal source. At first it might seem faint and crackly, but as you fine tune your receiver the signal will become crisper and clearer and you will be in no doubt that you are tuned in and making contact with your source. It is in this place that you will find guidance and direction. Here you can receive answers to all the questions or dilemmas that you might be facing.

23

MUDDY WATERS AND SOWING SEEDS

When the bed of the pool has been stirred up and the waters have become muddy, it is no good jumping into the water to try and fix it; the water will only become muddier.

Be still and wait, the mud will settle on its own and the waters will become clear again.

How many times in my life have I done exactly what I should not do at moments like this? When I've found myself either in, or simply observing a situation where there might be a problem, or a disagreement or misunderstanding and I have stepped in and opened my mouth. The motive and intention may well have been good and pure and I've tried to say something to defend or to calm the situation but it has only served to stir things up and make the water even muddier than it was before I waded in.

I don't always find it easy to keep my mouth shut, particularly if I see something that I consider to be unfair or if I witness someone being hurt by the words or attitude of another. On a couple of occasions recently I have found myself in a position where I have voiced my concerns only to find that my opinion has "rattled" somebody else and escalated something, and it would have been better had I not got involved. In one instance I felt that somebody was being unreasonably criticised and even falsely accused and so I spoke up in defence of the individual concerned, only to spark, what turned out to be, a very heated debate about freedom of speech which involved even more abusive and aggressive language. On another occasion I suggested that more consideration be given to providing disabled access and facilities at an event that was being organised. This resulted in one of the organisers taking it as a personal attack regarding the way they had been running the event for 4 years. Instead of backing off and keeping quiet, I thought I then had to defend myself and explain my reasons for my original suggestion. Again this resulted in the whole thing getting entirely out of hand so that, by the time I did back off, others had joined in and taken over the argument with any sense of reason thrown out of the window.

This is something of a difficult one to deal with. Certainly there are times when one needs to voice their opinion rather than sit back and allow injustice or bullying take place, but I am beginning to realise that it is a bit like working in the garden. Very often the seeds have to just be scattered over the ground and then gently covered over. Then all we have to do is leave them there and allow the sun and rain to do the rest whilst we sit back and watch the flowers grow. If we dig too deeply before placing the seeds and them cover them with too much soil, it is going to be a long time before we get to see the flower grow, if it ever grows at all.

By **Being Still** before we speak, rather than jumping in and making the waters muddier, we can then connect with the spirit within and know what to say, when to say it and, most importantly, when to keep quiet.

24
BE WILLING TO RECEIVE

If you were to walk down the street tomorrow and somebody stopped you and offered you a £50 note, you would probably be very surprised. You might view them with suspicion, you might think they were mad or that the note was perhaps a forgery, or even stolen. You might think you were on *Candid Camera*. In a situation like this you really have two options; you can just keep on walking and ignore this strange individual, or you could say thank you, hold out your hand and allow him to give you the £50. If you keep on walking, you will be no worse off than you were when you left the house, if, on the other hand however, you accept the gift you will find yourself £50 better off than you were 5 minutes before.

I remember an old story that I was once told, about a very religious man who when out sailing found himself in the middle of a very violent storm, which blew him off course and smashed his boat onto some rocks. Throughout the storm he continued to believe that he would be safe and that god would deliver him. His boat was destroyed on the rocks and he managed to swim to safety and ended up on the shore of a desert island, miles from anywhere, with no food or fresh water. Still he had faith that his god would save him and all would be well. After a few days, when the weather had calmed, he saw a yacht on the horizon, the vessel came closer to the island and, not wanting to risk going to close to the rocks, the captain called out to the shipwrecked sailor suggesting that he swim out to the yacht and be taken to safety.

"No, it's alright, god will save me, I'll stay here until he does"

A couple of days later, the sailor was tired and weak from lack of food or drink, but still keeping his faith. From the sky he heard a noise which seemed to be getting louder he looked up and saw a helicopter. With no space to land, the pilot let down a rope ladder for the sailor to climb to his safety.

Once again the sailor called out, *"It's ok, I know that god is going to save me, I won't have to wait much longer"*

On two more occasions passing boats tried in vain to get the shipwrecked sailor to leave the island and swim to safety, but still he held on to his belief that god would save him.

Finally the sailor died from starvation. Presenting himself at the gates of heaven he asked god, *"Why didn't you save me? I believed that you would but you left me to die"*

"I wanted to save you but you wouldn't let me," replied god, *"I sent you three boats and a helicopter, but each time you refused the help that was offered."*

Be clear about this, nothing is ever forced on you. What you don't receive, you don't have.

So often, we fail to realise the abundance of life that the universe offers us because our ears, eyes and mind are closed to what is actually on offer. Sometimes we are just too proud or stubborn to receive. We need to accept what is given to us, otherwise it isn't ours. Accept the small things, the gratitude of others, the little gifts. If you find a penny on the street, pick it up, be grateful for it – it may only be 1 penny, but that's what pounds are made of.

And remember not to be too busy asking, praying, searching, so busy that you fail to see what is being offered.

Be Still, and be aware, be mindful and you will see the manifestation of abundance in your life.

This principle of receiving also works with the negative things in life. You only have what you receive. Refuse to accept the pain in your back. Refuse to accept the negative comments that you might hear. Refuse to accept illness. Refuse to accept hardship. Refuse to accept negativity.

What you don't receive, you don't have, whether it is good or bad.

25

A TIME OF UNLEARNING

From the moment we are born, we hear and see so many things that over the years have taken root in our subconscious. There are so many things that we have been told and taught that are now buried deep in our psyche, some are good, some are not so good. In order to achieve some sort of communion and oneness with the universe or with spirit, there is much of what we have learnt that we now have to unlearn, to forget, and to move away from.

Maybe you were told that your god is a jealous and judgemental god. That when you die you may have to face the prospect of eternal damnation. You could well have been told that we are all separated from god and so need a saviour to restore any relationship with the divine. The idea that, as a father I would punish my children if they didn't live their lives in the way that I wanted, or did not believe every word I said, by locking them up in the cellar and then throwing away the key, is absurd. Yet this is what many religious leaders tell us that their father god does not hesitate to do by sending unbelievers to hell for eternity.

You might have been told to "look after number one". Or maybe that some people are more important than others, and you are not worthy or deserving of good things.

Were you ever told that society was made up of those who have and those who have not, and that you were destined to be amongst the latter?

Perhaps you are from a generation that was told that male and female were different – girls played at "making home" while boys did all the rough stuff. Certainly you were told that "big boys don't cry".

If you now find it hard to trust people, that could well be because as a child you were always taught to be wary and suspicious of strangers. It is interesting to note that most crimes against children are committed by family members or friends of the family, as opposed to complete strangers.

In the Western world we live in a society that is blighted by fear, mistrust, greed and selfishness – all because of the things we learnt while we were growing up.

The time has arrived for us to put aside so much of what lies in our unconscious and to wake up to a new way of living. A way that acknowledges that we are all part and parcel of the same universe. That we are not, and never have been separated, that there is no judgment, that the world is not an evil place populated by people who are out to get you. And knowing this, it is our responsibility to ensure that we do not continue to feed this damaging misinformation to those around us and to those who have been entrusted into our care.

Be Still, go inside yourself and just be. Experience that deep inner peace, trust yourself, trust what you sense. Know that you are connected to all that is. **Be Still** and be at one with the universe. And by being at one with the universe, know that you are at one with everything and everyone who is also part of that universe.

It really is so simple. You can't change the world overnight, but you can change your life, change your thinking, change your programming. As you, as an individual, come to a realisation that you are one with all that is around you, that you have a connection with everyone you meet or come into contact with, no matter how briefly that may be, then your life will become more peaceful. You will understand how pointless criticism is, how ridiculous it is to argue or to insist that your opinion is right – why would you argue or be in conflict with your self? You see, that's what this whole concept of "oneness" and non-duality is about, we are all different parts of the one whole, and as such we really are all one.

26

AUTOMATIC TRANSMISSION

Not long ago I purchased a new car. I had always driven quite large vehicles, either estate cars or vans, mainly due to my work as a musician and the need to transport sound equipment, but now felt it was time to downsize to a smaller model, which would be more environmentally friendly. I eventually found one that suited me at a very good price but, unlike my previous cars this one had an automatic transmission and I have to say, I love it! During nearly 40 years of driving I never really did like the manual shift gears, so to sit behind the wheel of a car and just let it go, without having to think about changing gears is fantastic. I just put it in drive and away we go. No more crunching, no more worrying about damaging the clutch, just sit back and drive.

When we connect directly to the energy source, or to spirit, it is a bit like driving an automatic transmission vehicle. We trust that when a gear needs to change, it just does and when it does, you can feel the shift. As you relax into your connection with the divine, you realise that you don't actually have to do anything. When it is time for you to move into another gear, you really will be aware of the shift taking place, all you need to do is to go with it, feel the change and relax into that new awareness.

On occasion, when driving, we may have a tendency to change gear too soon or at the wrong time, resulting in a rather uncomfortable crunching sound. This doesn't happen in an automatic car and it doesn't happen when we are living in a state of spiritual connection or alignment. Those occasions when we try and move into something before we are actually ready, seem to happen less frequently and we find that the shift only takes place at the right time. Being connected to, and trusting in, the universal driving force, eliminates the crunching and the burning out of the clutch as we move through the gears on our journey to oneness or enlightenment.

Be Still, connect to the source, sit back, follow the road and enjoy the ride.

27

AT THE THIRD STROKE

The time will be precisely,

.   .   .   .   .

Now.

As you breathe, there will only ever be one time and that time is now. Wherever you are, whatever you are doing, whomever you are with, the only time is now. What you perceive as the past was actually "*now*" when you were experiencing it. What you believe to be the future will be "*now*" when you are actually there.

We spend so much time thinking about the past, how we might have done things differently, said things differently, taken a different route. All these thoughts are totally pointless. The past has gone, it doesn't exist any more than the future exists, so there is not really a lot of point in worrying about that either!

When we put so much attention on the past or the future we are neglecting to put our attention into the present, the now, and as a result we are missing out on all that now has to offer us. We cannot change the past and we cannot be fully aware of what the future might have in store, all we can really know is what is happening now. It makes no sense whatsoever to give our energy to anything other than now.

Be still, concentrate on your breathing, breathe slowly and deeply and be mindful of the present, the now. Now is all the time you have and now you have all the time. If thoughts of the past or the future come into your mind, acknowledge them and put them aside as you bring your attention back to your breathing and to the present. Be grateful for the things that have happened in the past, things that have brought you to this place where you are now, but don't dwell on them. Don't let them fill your mind. Be mindful of now.

This present moment is special, it is unique, it is totally different from any other moment – it is now. Enjoy it and live in it, experiencing all the beauty of the moment, accepting all the blessings of now. Immerse yourself in the moment – nothing else matters, nothing else is real. This moment is all you have, it is everything – it is now.

28

RESPECT THE VALUE

Let's not waste time beating about the bush here but get straight to the point on this one – I have been a practising Therapist for some time now, working primarily in the realm of Sound Healing and it has been very clear to me during this time that the majority of practising Therapists do not charge anywhere near enough for the treatments they are offering!

Your health, be it physical, mental, emotional, or spiritual, is probably the most important and valuable thing you possess. Yet, for some unknown reason, so many of us still regard having some sort of Health Treatment as a luxury, something to pamper ourselves with.

As I spend a lot of time having to drive around the country, I have to ensure that my vehicle is safe and road-worthy. That means that, like all car owners, I have to ensure that my car has regular services at my local garage. According to The Times newspaper back in 2008, the average hourly rate for a garage mechanic was £75.17. Now, my local garage doesn't charge me that amount, but I regularly pay around £50 an hour for labour - that doesn't take into account any parts, oil etc., the "treatment" is charged on top of that rate. We value our vehicles, many of us depend on them - how much more should we value our own bodies and our health and wellbeing?

At the time of writing, Her Majesty's Courts Service guidelines recommend that solicitors' charges in South Wales should be in the region of somewhere between £111 and £201 an hour.

If you are lucky enough to have an NHS Dentist, a 15-minute check up will cost you £16.50 - that's £66 an hour. If not, and you see a private dentist, the going rate is £43, an amazing £172 an hour.

Now, I'm not suggesting that we should be paying or charging so much for Complementary Health treatments, but I am saying that both the client and the Therapist need to start being realistic and to put a real value on what can produce life-changing benefits.

Too many Complementary Therapists cheapen themselves and their skills by putting too low a value on what they have to offer. When was the last time you saw a private hospital offering "two operations for the price of 1", or "discount pamper days"? It just doesn't happen. Yet if you believe in the benefits of the therapies you are offering, why treat your practice as if it is a discount warehouse?

There is also a very negative attitude amongst some Therapists who say that "if I charge more than a certain amount, people won't come". You know, I'm going to let you into a secret now - that just isn't true! I recently heard of a Therapist who didn't like offering a particular treatment so decided to double the amount they were charging for that treatment, thinking it would put people off. It actually had the opposite effect with the result that she had more work than ever with clients believing that they get what they pay for.

Two people were overheard talking in a waiting room about complementary treatments, one was heard to say, *"I had a treatment, it was really good - cost me £30"*. Her companion very proudly replied, *"Oh, I paid £40 for mine, it was wonderful"*. Understand Therapists, if you don't place a real value on your skills and work, neither will your clients.

What should we be charging or paying for treatments? Let's try and be totally realistic and practical here. In order for the Therapist to earn what is the average yearly salary in the UK which, according to the Daily Telegraph in November 2011, was £26,200 there are a number of things that need to be taken into consideration.

If you are reading this as a Therapist, the main thing you need to consider is the cost of being a Therapist, the overheads and expenses incurred in running a Complementary Therapy practice. If you are reading this as a client, you also should be aware of the costs involved. Add up how much is being spent per year on things such as room rental, advertising, business *cards, fliers etc., insurance, membership of regulatory bodies and associations, costs of further training and Continuing Professional* Development (we are not going to even consider the thousands of pounds spent on initial training to qualify as a Therapist), business stationery, telephone charges, equipment (massage couch, couch rolls, candles, oils etc., depending on the therapy being offered). On top of that you should add on at least 10% so that some profit can be made to put back into the business. Finally, add that figure to the average salary figure we mentioned earlier.

Now work out how many hours can realistically be

worked in actually treating clients in a day and how many days can be worked in a week.

Next, work out how many weeks a year will be worked, after taking into account holidays, bank holidays etc.

Multiply the number of weeks that can be worked, by the number of clients that can be treated in a week.

Divide the total of the expenses, profit and salary by the number of hourly clients that can be treated in a year, and this will give you an idea of how much you should be charging, or paying, per hour. Don't be surprised to find that it is a lot more than the amount being charged at the moment. And that is if the Therapist just wants to be "average" on an average income!

So remember, value yourself, value your health and value the time and expertise of those who offer their skills and therapeutic treatments.

Having read the above, take time now to **Be Still** and consider how much you value your health. Consider how much you value those who have trained and studied in order to offer their expertise and skill in providing therapies and treatments.

*

I've concentrated on therapies and Therapists in this chapter, but everything I have said can be applied to whatever skill you have to offer or make use of, be it accounting, cleaning, waiting tables, teaching, caring or any skill or service you can think of. Value yourself and value those who serve you.

29

LAUGHING MATTERS

When I was about 12 years old, somebody bought my parents a subscription to The Reader's Digest. Every month, for a year, it would be delivered to us and I would gain great pleasure from going straight to the regular columns such as, *Word Power, Humour in Uniform, Life's Like That and my favourite, Laughter, The Best Medicine.*

I more recently discovered the truth of laughter being the best medicine, when I discovered Laughter Yoga and enrolled on a course to train as a Laughter Yoga Leader. I hadn't realised that so much research had actually been done into how laughter can actually have a direct effect on our health and wellbeing. For instance a recent study into the treatment of leg ulcers at Leeds University discovered that the simplest treatment was the most effective – a good laugh. It was found that actual physiological changes occurred as a result of laughter which assisted in healing the ulcers. Professor Andrea Nelson who led the study said: *"Believe it or not, having a really hearty chuckle can help. This is because laughing gets the diaphragm moving and this plays a vital part in moving blood around the body."*

Laughter not only provides a full-scale workout for your muscles, it unleashes a rush of stress-busting endorphins. And what is even more amazing is that your body can't distinguish between real and fake laughter! This is one area of life where faking it is just as good as the real thing. The feeling you get when you laugh is a fantastic way of combating the physical effects of stress. When we laugh, endorphins, which are the natural opiates or painkillers produced by our bodies, are released into the blood stream.

It has also been shown that the level of natural killer cells (a type of immune cell that attacks virus and tumour cells) is increased through laughter. Research indicates that just 20 seconds of laughter could be as good for the cardiovascular system as three minutes spent on a rowing machine. Scientists found that laughing heartily causes the endothelium, the tissue that forms the inner lining of the blood vessels, to dilate, increasing the blood flow in the same way as a bout of aerobic exercise, but without the aches, pains and muscle tension sometimes associated with exercise.

Laughter lowers blood pressure, boosts immune function and triggers the release of endorphins in the brain, which produce a sense of wellbeing. When you have a good hearty laugh, every organ in your body, your heart, your lungs, the digestive system, is being massaged.

We can all benefit from a good laugh, young or old, in groups or on our own. It has been shown that mental health patients are likely to especially benefit from laughter therapy. It is an interesting fact that on average, young children laugh about

400 times a day whereas adults only manage a miserable 15.

Laughing is something that we can do at any time – not just when we are happy. Laughing when stressed or angry, even if it is fake laugher, can lift your mood. And of course, laughter is infectious, those of you old enough to remember Norman Wisdom will know that he didn't even need to tell a joke to get his audience laughing – he just laughed and we all joined in.

Not only is laughter good for physical health it is also extremely beneficial to our spiritual health. Sometimes we take life and spirituality too seriously. Humans have been blessed with the ability to laugh, it is a gift and a very important part of our make up, which provides enormous and important benefits. Next time something happens in your life which causes you stress or discomfort, frustration or hurt, why not try taking a deep breath and then letting out a hearty belly laugh – you might look stupid, but believe me it really does work and will help you to feel better.

Be Still, look inside yourself and ask if you take life too seriously. Do you allow pressures and stressful situations to pull you down? Make a decision to see the funny side, and if you can't see it – laugh anyway. Remember that your brain cannot distinguish between real and fake laughter and will start to produce endorphins, which will start to make you feel happier and better straight away. Laughter really is the best medicine.

30

SPIRITUALITY OR RELIGION

Religion is often defined as any formal or institutional expression of a belief in, worship of, or obedience to, a supernatural power considered to be divine or to have control of human destiny. The practice of sacred ritual observances, sacred rites or ceremonies.

The word *"religion"* comes to us via Old French from the Latin *religiō* fear of the supernatural, piety, probably from *religāre* to tie up, from re- + *ligāre* to bind.

Spirituality, however, is defined as the state or quality of being dedicated to spiritual things or values, especially as contrasted with material or temporal ones.

I think that the best way that I can describe the difference between religion and spirituality, is to say that religion is outward while spirituality is inward.

I don't particularly want to get into the argument that says that the majority of wars are caused by religion, because I don't really believe that to be the case – the majority of wars are actually caused by fear, greed and power, of wanting to have more, and to have power over others and their property. Now I know that those words can be used to describe some religions or religious leaders, but to blame religion for all of the world's disputes is stretching things a little bit too far.

It is my belief that religion and spirituality do not necessarily go hand in hand, I would even go so far as to say that religion is actually often a hindrance to spirituality. Over the years there have been many great and inspired teachers, prophets, and avatars whose teachings have been turned into religions. If we look closely at all of these religions we can see that there is very little connection between the original teachings that they claim to be based on and the religious organisation that we see today.

Jesus told his followers not to store up material treasures, but to give away, to share with those who had need – yet so many Christian churches and cathedrals are furnished and decorated with priceless pieces of art and precious metals, whilst millions starve. Francis of Assisi, turned his back on material things and gave all his possessions to the poor, yet he is remembered in Assisi today by the construction of a fantastic basilica. There is something obscene about this memorial to a man who would have despised such a thing.

But it's not just Christianity that should come under the microscope. The Buddha, like St Francis, turned his back on all things material in order to reach enlightenment. Yet if we look at some of the amazing Buddhist temples with their statues of gold and precious stone, it is hard to relate this to the man who found his truth sitting under a tree. We just have to look around at some of the places of worship of all organised religions and see the contradiction between the teachings and the practice.

So much of religion is about the outward show. Christian churches were built in a spirit of competition, it was important to have the tallest spire in order to be seen from the furthest distance away. The majority of religions are about power, power of men over the common people. Power enforced by rules and regulations laid down by the leaders of those religions. Power enforced by ritual and practices. Whether it is Judaism, Christianity, Islam, Buddhism, Krishna Consciousness, Neo-Paganism or any other brand of religion, there are those who are part of the particular religious hierarchy, who lay down the law as to what must be done to achieve salvation or enlightenment. As we have seen from the origin of the word "*religion*", it is about bondage, being tied, imprisoned.

Spirituality, on the other hand, has none of this. Spirituality is about having a direct connection and relationship with the spiritual, which is not dependant on the material world and not dependant on priests or other representatives of the light. Spirituality is about one's own personal awareness of the source of all things and a commitment to living in that awareness. There is no-one to tell you how it should be done, no-one to tell you what you should say, and no-one to tell you how you should live. By simply making that connection in your own heart, your spirit to the one spirit, you will know what to do, what to say and how to live. Unlike religion, spirituality is about freedom.

It is a wonderful thing to be able to share with others on your spiritual path, particularly to spend time with those who share a similar belief or ethic, but once you try to organise that sharing, it becomes a thing of ego and of power. The spiritual aspect, if not washed away totally, is certainly diluted.

Many religions are based on written scriptures and texts, and although some claim these books to be the *"word of god"*, we need to remember that they are just books, written by men. Some of the writings may indeed be inspirational and edifying, but they are just opinions and interpretations, as are all writings, including the words you are reading now. If the Bible is the word of god, then god must have been very confused when he "channelled" it through the writers. Each of the four gospels contains a different account of the crucifixion of Jesus, and many other stories would seem to contradict each other. This is only to be expected, if you ask four people to describe an event that they witnessed, you are going to get four different accounts, depending on their viewpoint. If this really is the word of god, I'm sure he would have kept to the same story. And how do you decide between the Bible, the Koran and the Bhagavad Gita? Each one is claimed by its disciples to be the word of god, yet they are all so very different.

The opening verse of the Tao Te Ching says, *"The Tao that can be named is not the Tao"*. Yes, I know it's just another book of wise sayings, but I am inclined to think that any book, religion, or teacher who names their way the "truth", you will more than likely find that it is not, in fact the truth. If they say that their way is the right way, it is probably the wrong way.

The Buddha, Gautama Siddharta, is reported as saying, over 2,500 years ago:

"Do not believe in anything simply because you have heard it. Do not believe in anything simply because it is spoken and rumoured by many. Do not believe

in anything simply because it is found written in your religious books. Do not believe in anything merely on the authority of your teachers and elders. Do not believe in traditions because they have been handed down for many generations. But after observation and analysis, when you find that anything agrees with reason and is conducive to the good and benefit of one and all, then accept it and live up to it."

It is good to listen to the words of wise teachers, whether written or spoken, and then to decide if they resonate with the spirit within. You have no need of someone to tell you how you should live as a spiritual entity, you have no need to follow a routine practice or ritual that someone has laid down for you, in order to find peace and contentment. You have no need to be a sheep and to mindlessly follow the flock. You have no need to practise endless disciplines in order to be one with the universe. You have no need of temples or cathedrals when you have the natural world around you, which speaks of the beauty and power of creation. Your temple can be a tree, the sea, your garden, your heart.

To discover and to live a life of spirituality, just look inside yourself and connect with the spirit within, which is connected to the one spirit. **Be still** and be aware. Listen to the spirit within and live accordingly, harming no one and no thing, but leaving peace and light in your trail, wherever you walk.

John Lennon's words in the song "Imagine" are probably very familiar to you but I would ask you to read them again, or listen to the song and ruminate on the words, and make the dream a reality in your own life. We can't change the world in an instant, but we can change our own world, and if each one of us was to do that, the world would indeed be a better place.

31

REST IN PEACE

It has always struck me as quite strange that we use the phrase *"Rest In Peace"* whenever somebody dies. Why wait until they are dead? One of the greatest discoveries that I have made is that it is possible to rest in peace while I am still alive, we don't have to wait until we are in the grave until we can find eternal peace.

Ok, I admit, part of us does have to die in order to find peace. That part of us that is always hungry for more, that is driven by greed, by the need for recognition. The part that is always searching for satisfaction. The part that is searching for self-knowledge, for enlightenment. Yes, even the part that is striving and searching to find peace.

One could sum all that up by saying that it is the ego that has to die.

Once we allow the ego to die, we are set free, free to live a higher existence, free to be one with the universe, one with god, to realise that we are god.

Free to rest in peace.

How do we do this? How do we allow the ego to die?

You've got it . . . .

Be Still.

Stop what you are doing.

Stop striving.

Stop struggling.

Stop rushing.

Stop striving to reach your goals, to achieve your dreams.

Stop trying to be someone or something that you are not.

Stop and Be Still.

Give up on all those false ideas that you hold in your subconscious.

Give up on believing in your separateness.

Give up and Be Still.

Be Still and be whole.

Be Still and be at one with the universe.

32

DEATH IS NOT THE END

This may seem strange to many readers but one of my greatest passions in life is death and everything that surrounds it. I am fascinated by the way we approach death in different societies, particularly Western society, the taboos surrounding death, the fears and hopes connected to death and the way we deal with the passing of those we love and care for. It has always seemed strange to me that the one thing that we can all be certain of, is the one thing that so many people find difficulty in preparing for and addressing. It is as if we have decided that if we don't talk about it, if we ignore it or sweep the subject under the carpet it won't happen.

Both of my parents died within 4 months of each other. My mother was diagnosed with cancer when she was in her early 70s and two weeks later my father was diagnosed with another form of cancer, non-Hodgkin lymphoma. That summer they celebrated their golden wedding anniversary, 50 years of sharing a happy life together and now together they were both facing coming to the end of their lives. The months between their diagnoses and their passing was a most precious time for me, and I felt privileged to be able to care for them both and share their thoughts and love.

Being self-employed, I was able to spend much of their last months back at home with them, travelling the 400 miles round trip at weekends to go back to my own home and keep an eye on things there, while my brother was able to spend a couple of days with them when he wasn't having to work.

My mother was a wonderful woman and it was very moving to witness her making plans for her own funeral, choosing the songs and readings that she wanted to be sung and read during the service. She knew exactly what she wanted and she wanted to have a hand in the planning. She loved my father very much and had devoted herself to looking after him as he had not been well for many years and had been forced to retire at an early age. I think we had all expected her to outlive my father and it was a surprise to see her deteriorating so quickly, she was naturally concerned about how Dad would cope without her.

Mum had requested that she spend her last days in a newly-opened hospice which was just across the road from their home, and towards the end she was heavily sedated. I had to go home for a couple of days but was half expecting to get a phone call to bring me back before I was due to return. However, when I did get back she was so heavily drugged up with pain killers that she was unable to communicate and lay on her bed in an unconscious state. We knew that the end of her life was near and Dad and I sat by her bed, glad that we could be with her and that she wasn't alone. I was sitting holding her hand and after some time she opened her eyes and looked at me. With a look of such peace and contentment in her eyes she silently mouthed the word goodbye and took her final breath. That was, and still is the most beautiful moment I have ever experienced. If ever I had had any questions or fears about dying, they all disappeared in that moment. I don't know what she saw or felt at that moment, maybe she was seeing loved ones that had gone on before, maybe it was her own daughter who had died as a baby, maybe it was a welcoming light – whatever it was I knew my mother was at peace and was ready to go.

One of the things that my mother had decided was that she wanted to be cremated and, believing that her body was simply a vehicle for her soul to inhabit in this life, had no particular preference as to what should be done with her ashes. Dad decided that Mum's ashes should be scattered at the crematorium. A few days after the funeral a thought came to me, too late to do anything about now though, that it would have been nice to have scattered her ashes on my sister's grave. Glenys was my parents' first born child and she had died when she was only a few months old. As I say, it was now too late to do so but I decided to visit my sister's grave as I felt I wanted to say to her *"look, we've had the joy of having Mum around all these years, and thank you for that, now it's your turn to be reunited with her"*.

It was just after the Second World War when Glenys died and Mum and Dad didn't have a lot of money so no memorial stone was ever erected on her grave. I could remember as a young boy visiting the plot every year on the anniversary of her death with my father to leave flowers, so I had a vague idea of where she was buried. In order to locate the exact spot I did have the advantage of knowing that she was buried next to another young child who was the son of friends of my parents. His name was Garth and he did have a memorial stone where he lay, so all I had to do was to locate Garth's grave and I would then find Glenys'. This was easier said than done, I don't know how many graves there are in Kettering cemetery but after nearly an hour of fruitless searching I was just about ready to give up. I had been all around the area that I thought I remembered, I had even been around an area that seemed to be set aside for the final resting place of children but I had been unable to find a stone with Garth's name engraved on it.

As I was about to leave the cemetery and give up the search, something happened that to this day I have only ever shared with a handful of people. I'm not what you might call a "cat-lover"; in fact throughout my life I have been plagued with an allergy to cats. I only have to be in a room where a cat has been and my throat starts to itch and my eyes start to water. Somehow, cats seem to sense this and make a decided effort to come and sit on my lap if ever I am in their company. As I started to make my way to the gate I noticed a cat starting to follow me, the cat then did something which I don't think is very normal for cats to do. It started nipping at my trouser leg with its teeth. It pulled at my hem and then would move back a few paces and sit and look at me. It did this 3 or 4 times as if it wanted me to follow it. Thinking to myself *"this is stupid"*, I followed the cat until it made itself comfortable and sat down on a grave. Was this it? Had this cat somehow led me to my sister's burial place? I went over to it and read the inscription on the stone and to my disappointment realised that it was not the one I had been searching for.

"This really is stupid", I said to myself and turned to leave. As I turned, there in front of me I read the name *"Garth Davidson"*. I had found it and right alongside was a small unmarked grave which was the resting place of my sister. I was able to say what I wanted to say and at the same time realise

that my mother had not really gone. I believe that somehow her spirit or energy had used that cat to guide me to where my sister's body lay.

When somebody we love and care for dies, we naturally mourn them, there is a gap that was once filled with their physical presence and that is hard for us to come to terms with and accept, but it is only the physical that has gone, the essence of that person remains. The basic laws of physics will tell us that energy cannot die. Energy continues to exist, it cannot be stopped, it has no beginning and it has no end. The word that describes this is *"eternal"*. We have all heard religions talking about the promise of eternal life if we live by certain rules, or worship a particular saviour. The truth is that the energy that is your life, that is my life, is eternal. It cannot be extinguished. Only the physical vessel that is our body passes away, the spirit, the energy, goes on.

Cast your mind back to the chapter on *"Connecting With The Energy"*, where we discussed the concept of there being only one energy, the source energy that we are all part of – the *"god energy"*. When our physical body dies, that *"god-energy"* continues, so in a sense everyone who has ever lived is still *"alive"*. This could perhaps account for those times when we feel the presence of those who have gone before, when we sense the closeness of loved ones that we have lost. I don't know and I don't claim to have all the answers but I do believe that we never truly lose someone, that something of them is always with us.

Be Still, spend some time in awareness of your connection with the god-energy of which you are a part and think about a loved one who is physically no longer with you. Be aware of them and their closeness to you. You might even smell a particular fragrance that you associate with them or even hear the sound of their voice in your mind. Only the body has gone, their essence, their life force, their spirit is still part of that energy to which you are connected and of which you also are a part. This could be a chance for you to say the things that you missed the opportunity to say while they were still with you in body. A chance to say *"thank you"*, or *"I'm sorry"*, a chance to say *"I love you"* or to forgive them. In the stillness you can still connect with them even though their physical presence is no longer around.

33
AND FINALLY . . .

Go placidly amid the noise and haste, and remember what peace there may be in silence.

You are a child of the universe, no less than the trees and the stars; you have a right to be here. And whether or not it is clear to you, no doubt the universe is unfolding as it should.

Therefore be at peace with God, whatever you conceive Him to be, and whatever your labours and aspirations, in the noisy confusion of life, keep peace in your soul.

With all its sham, drudgery and broken dreams, it is still a beautiful world.

(from Desiderata by Max Ehrmann)

Thanks and appreciation to the following people who have taught and inspired me over the years.

Dr Ern Baxter, Sid Purse, Ian Andrews, Ram Das, Dr Wayne D Dyer, Jacqueline Daly, Dr David Hamilton, Eckhart Tolle, Lama Geshe Abhay Rinpoche, Doreen Valiente, Cheryl Richardson and the multitude of others who have spoken words that have caused a light to shine.

Thanks also to Mary Jones for reading the manuscript and correcting my grammar and punctuation, and for the use of the kitchen table where much of this was written.

Grateful thanks to Kit Berry (Stonewylde) for her advice on the publishing process and also to Michael Reid for his technical support.

*

Special thanks and gratitude to my two daughters, Donna & Rhian who have taught me more than I can ever say, and to my partner and soul-mate Kiera for being patient and for supporting me with her love.

IF WE ARE FACING IN THE RIGHT DIRECTION, ALL WE HAVE TO DO IS KEEP ON WALKING

Jim Fox is an inspirational writer and speaker, based in South Wales. After spending many years as a professional musician, performing throughout the UK and Scandinavia, he trained as a Sound Therapist and, together with his wife, went on to open an Holistic Centre, providing various therapies and training & workshop facilities.

Jim is also joint editor of Labyrinth, *an online holistic magazine. He is married to Kiera and has two grown-up children.*

www.jimfox.info

www.thecentre-swansea.co.uk